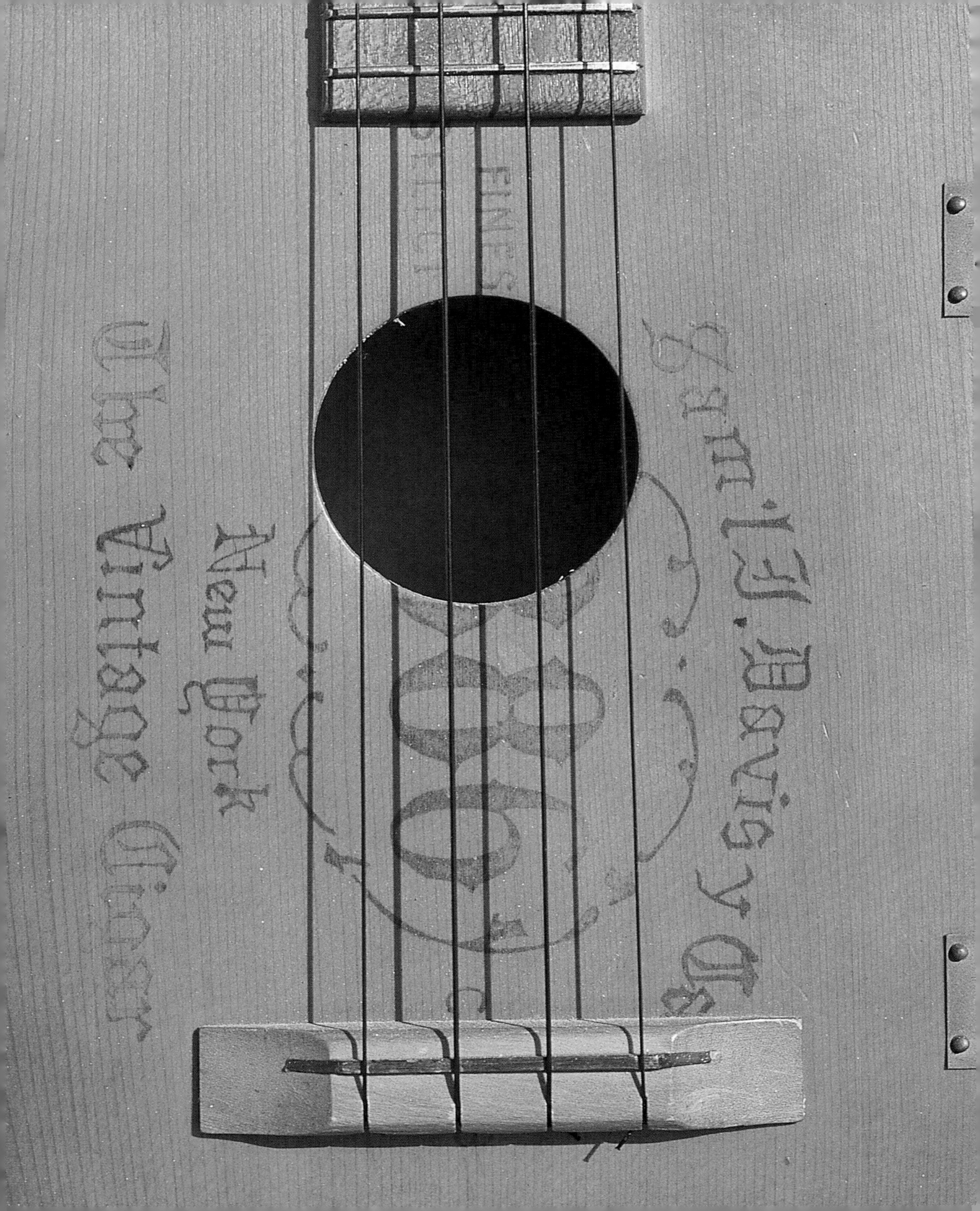

The UKULELE
A Visual History

BY

JIM BELOFF

REVISED & EXPANDED

Art Direction & Design
by TOMMY STEELE & ANDY ENGEL
Additional Design
by DOUG HAVERTY

Edited by RONNY S. SCHIFF

Backbeat
Books
San Francisco

AUTHOR'S ACKNOWLEDGMENTS

A number of people deserve mention for their help in making this book a reality.
For their eagle eyes, information, research materials, advice, encouragement and time,
a big "thank-you" goes out to Marvin and Gladys Beloff, George Chaltas, George Hinchliffe,
Brian Litman, Mike Longworth, Don and Audrey Maihock, Leonard Maltin, Chris Morris,
Andy Norwood, Poncie Ponce, Andy Roth, Lee Silva, Lyndon Smith, Tiny Tim,
Ian Whitcomb, Tim White, and ukulele fans around the world.
A big "mahalo" to all of my friends in Hawaii—Elma T. Cabral, Bob Gleason, David Hurd, Sam Jr.,
Fred and Chris Kamaka, Ohta-San, Lyle Ritz, Roy Sakuma, Dee Dee Wood, and Alan Yoshioka.
Also a special "thank you" to DeSoto Brown, Leslie Nunes, Gene Sculatti and
Paul Syphers for reading the manuscript with a red pencil and helping it, and me, look better.
A big nod of the "headstock" goes to Matt Kelsey and Backbeat Books for agreeing to share
this vision. Also to Tommy Steele and Andy Engel who put the "visual" in this history so magnificently.
And to my agent and editor Ronny Schiff, who has said "let's make book" more than four times now.
Finally, an "I couldn't have done it without you" to Chuck Fayne.
Thanks for your extraordinary passion, advice and enthusiasm for this project, and,
of course, your ukes. And the largest "ICHDIWY" to my wife and partner Liz,
who continues to help make this journey such a delight.

CMP
United Business Media

Revised & Expanded Edition published by Backbeat Books, 600 Harrison Street, San Francisco, California 94107. www.backbeatbooks.com.
Email: books@musicplayer.com. An imprint of the Music Player Network, Publishers of *Guitar Player*, *Bass Player*, *Keyboard*, and other magazines.
United Entertainment Media, Inc., a CMP Information company

Distributed to the book trade in the US and Canada by Publishers Group West, 1700 Fourth Street, Berkeley, CA 94710
Distributed to the music trade in the US and Canada by Hal Leonard Publishing, P.O. Box 13819, Milwaukee, WI 53213

Library of Congress Cataloging-in-Publication Data
Beloff, Jim, 1955–
    The ukulele : a visual history / by Jim Beloff.
        p. cm
    Includes bibliographical references (p.) and index.
    ISBN 0-87930-758-7 (alk. paper)
    1. Ukulele. 2. Ukulele–Pictorial works. I. Title.
ML1015.U5B45 2003
787.8'919'09–dc21   20033052208

03 04 05 06 07   5 4 3 2 1
Photography: Tommy Steele, Clinton Ashton, Design: Andy Engel, Production Assistance: Kim Sanders, Lon Shapiro
The ukuleles on the following pages are courtesy of The Chuck Fayne Collection: 12, 15 (Dias), 65, 68, 78, 79, 80, 81, 82, 83
(Kamaka cigar box; painted pineapple), 85, 86, 87, 89, 90, 92, 93, 97 (Harmony airplane; mando-uke), 98 (Stella), 100, 101,
102–103 (all but Weissenborn), 104, 106, 125 (Eibert harp-uke).

Printed in China

The
UKULELE
A Visual History

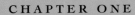

CHAPTER THREE

The Great Ukulele Manufacturers

ents

CHAPTER FOUR

The Story Continues ...

Introduction to the New Edition

When the first edition of *The Ukulele: A Visual History* was published in 1997, the ukulele was just beginning to appear again on the pop-culture radar. Six years later I'm happy to report that the ukulele is in the midst of a genuine renaissance, a true third wave of popularity. Ukulele festivals are happening all over the U.S. Mainland, songbooks for the ukulele are once again plentiful, fine new ukulele makers are setting up shops throughout Hawaii and the Mainland and a whole new crop of uke artists and virtuosos are "strumming their stuff." For ukulele players and fans these are exciting times.

Personally, it has been a very exciting time as well. In 1998, my wife, Liz, and I decided to make Flea Market Music, Inc. a full-time ukulele business. As of 2003 we've published 13 Jumpin' Jim's ukulele songbooks, produced the *Legends of Ukulele* compilation CD for Rhino Records and made a how-to-play video entitled *The Joy of Uke*. In 1999, my brother-in-law, Dale Webb, designed the FLUKE, a colorful, low-cost and uniquely shaped ukulele that has won admirers all over the world. In November 1999 my concerto for ukulele and symphony orchestra, *Uke Can't Be Serious,* was performed with the Wallingford (Connecticut) Symphony. In 2002, Liz and I were lead consultants on *Ukulele Fever* at the Stamford (Connecticut) Museum.

This new edition is a chance to improve upon the first-edition in three primary ways. Thanks especially to Hawaiian music historian, John King, we've made some small but critical changes to the first edition text regarding the Portuguese ancestor of the ukulele and its earliest days after arriving in Hawaii. Secondly, we've featured new players, new uke makers, new books and periodicals, as well as recent pop-culture visibility. Finally, here was an excuse to include more images of fun and unique new and vintage ukes. Thanks, especially, to Backbeat Books for allowing us the opportunity to revisit and update this volume. So far this whole ukulele adventure has been a wonderful and entirely unexpected ride. Every day we hear from folks who have discovered or rediscovered the joys of playing the ukulele and were delightfully changed by the encounter.

This has led us to believe more than ever that "Uke Can Change The World."

The ukulele community at large is unusually supportive and helpful. Many thanks go to all of the fine folks who have purchased this book over the years and volunteered additional info and images. Special thanks to Doug Haverty for helping with the "visual" in this new edition. Additional thanks to: Robert Armstrong, Clinton Ashton, Liz Beloff, Dick Boak, Don Blair, Mike Chock, Jean & Chalmers Doane, Tom Favilla, Chuck Fayne, Frank Ford, Travis Harrelson, Richard Johnston, Kenji Kawai, Matt Kelsey, Randy Klimpert, Matt Kobayashi, Maria Maccaferri, Amy Miller, Sandor Nagyszalanczy, John Nelson, Rosa Portell, Bill Robertson, Ronny Schiff, Michael Simmons, Tiki King, Jason Verlinde and Stan Werbin.

Keep on strummin'!

FLEA MARKET
MUSIC, INC.
BOX 1127
STUDIO CITY,
CALIFORNIA 91614

www.fleamarketmusic.com

THE FOUR DIFFERENT SIZES OF UKE.
FROM LEFT TO RIGHT: SOPRANO 21", CONCERT 25", TENOR 26 1/4", BARITONE 30 3/4"
THE SOPRANO IS THE MOST COMMON SIZE.
THE BARITONE IS TUNED EXACTLY LIKE THE TOP FOUR STRINGS OF A GUITAR (D G B E).
THE SOPRANO, CONCERT AND TENOR ARE USUALLY TUNED G C E A,
WITH THE G AN OCTAVE UP, RESULTING IN THE FAMOUS "MY DOG HAS FLEAS" TUNING.
(PHOTO BY ELIZABETH MAIHOCK BELOFF)

f *w*
o *o*
r *r*
e *d*

Thanksgiving 1995 will be remembered as a high-water mark in the ongoing history of the ukulele. During the three-night television broadcast of *The Beatles Anthology* documentary, the ukulele received an unusual amount of visibility. Paul McCartney referred to John Lennon's mom, who played the uke, and offered that "to this day, if I ever meet grownups who play ukuleles, I love 'em." Later on, George Harrison is shown playing "I Will" on a uke as well as a never-recorded tune. All of this attention coming from a musical group who made every kid in the world want to play the guitar. Could it be possible that, somehow, the ukulele was "cool" again?

For many of its fans, the ukulele has never been out of style. For players and collectors it is the subject of great passion. The inspiration behind this particular homage to the ukulele is twofold: As a uke collector, the first is a desire to have a comprehensive collection of photographs of the finest ukuleles ever made, as well as many examples of the great novelty ukes. The other driving force behind this book is simply that there hasn't been anything like it available to this day. With that in mind, this book is an attempt to pull together the whole story of the ukulele. Inside you will find the history of the uke, its most noteworthy players and personalities, the great manufacturers and a look at the current uke scene. What follows is truly a labor of love. If you have as much fun reading through this book as I had putting it together, I will consider it a job well done.

JOHN LENNON AND GEORGE HARRISON IN WAIKIKI.
FROM THE COLLECTION OF DESOTO BROWN.

CHAPTER ONE

The Birth — A Gift from Portugal

The ukulele is actually the descendant of a four-stringed musical instrument known as the *machête* or, less accurately, the *braguinha* from the Portuguese island of Madeira.

The collision of cultures that created the uke can be traced to the very specific date of August 23rd, 1879. This was the day that the *The History of the Ukulele* Ravens-crag, a British ship filled with 423 men, women and children from Madeira, arrived in Honolulu, Hawaii. After a difficult four month voyage, the weary travelers were understandably thrilled to have finally reached their destination. According to legend, upon arriving in Honolulu Harbor, a musician-passenger by the name of João Fernandes hopped onto the wharf and then began

MACHÊTE—THE BODY OF THE MACHÊTE
IS ABOUT 8 INCHES LONG, AND ITS FOUR CATGUT STRINGS
ARE TUNED D G B D. ONE HAWAIIAN OBSERVER NOTED
THAT THE MACHÊTE RESEMBLED A "PINE BOX WITH
SCALE MARKS ALL THE WAY DOWN TO THE HOLE, AND THE
TOP LEFT UNPOLISHED."

—

MAP—THE VOYAGE ROUTE FROM MADEIRA,
AROUND SOUTH AMERICA TO HAWAII.

—

HONOLULU HARBOR, CIRCA 1881, WITH A SHIP
SIMILAR TO THE RAVENSCRAG THAT BROUGHT
THE MACHÊTE TO HAWAII.
COURTESY OF THE BISHOP MUSEUM.

singing Portuguese folksongs of thanksgiving for their safe arrival. Although he was playing chiefly for the benefit of his fellow passengers, the assembled Hawaiians couldn't help but be moved by his performance. They also couldn't help but notice the curious instrument on which he was accompanying himself—a machête.

As fate would have it, three of the men on board the *Ravenscrag*, Augusto Dias, Manuel Nunes and José do Espirito Santo were talented craftsmen. All three were cabinet makers and Santo and Dias were both talented musicans. These three men would soon play a role in the development and popularization of the modern-day ukulele.

The Jumping Flea

There are many theories about how the ukulele got its name. The two most-circulated stories include one about an English army officer, Edward Purvis, who arrived in Hawaii in 1879. Purvis was a talented musician who became quite adept at playing the machête, and after being appointed Assistant Chamberlain to the court of King David Kalakaua, often entertained the court with his expert playing. Because he was small and sprightly (as opposed to the markedly larger frames of the Hawaiians), he was nicknamed "Ukulele," which in Hawaiian means "jumping flea" (also translated as "bouncing flea" and "leaping flea"). One theory suggests that Purvis' nickname simply spread to the instrument he loved to play.

A more literal theory likens the fingers of an accomplished player flying nimbly up and down the

EDWARD PURVIS (CIRCA 1880),
THE ORIGINAL "JUMPING FLEA."
PHOTO BY J. WILLIAMS,
BISHOP MUSEUM.

A Poor Prophecy

In 1850, John A. Dix, a U.S. Senator from New York, published a book entitled *A Winter In Madeira and a Summer in Spain and Florence.* In this book, Dix describes the *machête de braga,* the Portuguese ancestor of the ukulele, in this way: "It is an invention of the island, and one of which the island has no great cause to be proud. Its music, by itself, is thin and meagre; but in the streets at night, with a guitar or violincello accompaniment, it is very pretty." Dix goes on to say that despite a few good local *machête* players, he can't help but think how much better they would sound on a guitar—"in all respects a finer instrument." He concludes by saying, "It is not probable that the *machête* will ever emigrate from Madeira."
Ouch!

fretboard of the machête to the movement of "jumping fleas." Queen Lili'uokalani didn't care for this interpretation. She preferred a more poetic translation of the Hawaiian word *uku* as "the gift" and *lele* "to come," referring to the way in which this now-cherished instrument had come from Portugal to Hawaii (obviously the Hawaiian word "uku" has multiple meanings).

While there are many possible explanations as to the genesis of the ukulele's name, it is important to note that there is only one correct pronunciation in Hawaii: "oo-koo-le-le," which is in marked contrast to the way the "you-koo-le-le" is commonly pronounced on the Mainland.

The Ukulele Comes of Age

Although responding to a call for workers in Hawaii's sugar plantations, Augusto Dias expected to find employment in the woodworking industry. Like Fernandes, Dias was also a fine musician and reportedly passed the time on the *Ravenscrag* playing the guitar and singing. When Dias arrived in Honolulu in August of 1879, he was crushed to learn that most of the men from the ship were engaged as laborers in the fields. At ten dollars per month, Dias worked hard enough to pay off the year-long contract three months early.

With local interest growing in the machête, Dias, Nunes and Santo eventually opened their own instrument shops in Honolulu. Dias is listed in the 1884 City Directory and both he and Nunes advertised themselves as "machet" makers in an 1885 edition of the Portuguese-language newspaper *O Luso Hawaiiano*. In 1886 there is an article in the same paper about Santo's shop.

While there is more about Dias, the ukulele maker, in the third chapter, Dias the musician developed a long-standing relationship with King Kalakaua. Engaged regularly to perform at social functions at Iolani Palace, Dias would demonstrate his unique Spanish style of picking the melody, as opposed to using the instrument to just strum the chords. The King also held weekly poker parties where notables such as Robert Louis Stevenson would play his flageolet (a kind of recorder) and Dias would play the uke.

ABOVE: AUGUSTO DIAS
(COURTESY OF ELMA T. CABRAL)
ABOVE LEFT: MANUEL NUNES
(COURTESY OF LESLIE NUNES)
TWO OF THE THREE MADEIRAN MEN
WHO ARE CONSIDERED THE EARLY
DEVELOPERS OF THE UKULELE.
—
CENTER: SANTO UKE.
(COURTESY OF BILLY D. VOIERS),
PHOTO BY
ELIZABETH MAIHOCK BELOFF
—
FAR LEFT: A UKULELE MADE BY
AUGUSTO DIAS (1842-1915)

The Ukulele Finds a Patron

A key reason for the rapid acceptance of the ukulele was due to the patronage of Hawaii's "Merry Monarch," King David Kalakaua. His is an essential part of the story, not only because of the influence that he wielded, but also because he was a composer who happened to love to play the ukulele.

As a child, along with his brother and two sisters, Kalakaua was adopted by various members of the High Chief's family. From his grand-

KING DAVID KALAKAUA (1836-1891) ENTERTAINED MANY DISTINGUISHED VISITORS, INCLUDING ROBERT LOUIS STEVENSON, CENTER. COURTESY OF *PARADISE OF THE PACIFIC.*

mother he learned about the ancient Hawaiian music, and he learned about contemporary music through his teachers at the Royal School. He played piano, accordion, guitar and later, of course, the ukulele. David and his two sisters, the future Queen Lili'uokalani, Princess Likelike and his brother Prince Leleiohoku all became accomplished songwriters. Their talents, in fact, created a certain competitive spirit between them, leading to regular songwriting contests.

By 1882, the royal family's Iolani Palace was the nexus of Hawaiian dance, music and culture. The King's influence was such that after he learned to play the ukulele, he added a lilting rhythm to the traditional hula. It has been reported that he even learned to design and build his own ukuleles from Augusto Dias.

QUEEN LILI'UOKALANI, COMPOSER OF "ALOHA OE," ALSO PLAYED THE UKULELE.

Because the ukulele became King Kalakaua's favorite instrument, he made every effort to include it in all of his musical activities. According to legend, during the King's Jubilee celebration in 1886, the ukulele accompanied the hula dances for the first time. Thanks again to the King's patronage, the ukulele began to be a featured part of the instrumental ensembles of the leading glee clubs, and it was even written into the music of the royal composers.

While the enthusiasm of the royal family had a lot to do with the acceptance of the uke, it wasn't the whole story. The flames were also fanned by the fact that, in its redesign, the machête was evolving into an easier-to-play ukulele. Part of this evolution included increasing the size and altering the shape slightly and changing the tuning to allow for easier chord formation.

Between the years of 1880 and 1915, most ukulele-related activity was occurring in Hawaii. Nonetheless, as early as 1892, the ukulele was beginning to show up in various major cities on the Mainland.

From Hawaii With Love

The seeds of the Hawaiian tourism industry were sown as early as the 1880s, even before a group of businessmen overthrew the Hawaiian monarchy in 1893. Soon after, in 1900, Hawaii was admitted as a U.S. territory, and the Merchants Association of Hawaii was already looking seriously at ways to encourage visitors to the islands. In addition to the extraordinary beauty of their home, these early promoters were well aware of the powerful drawing power of Hawaiian dance and music. Symbolically, the bewitching maiden in a grass skirt and lei, strumming a ukulele, covered a lot of ground. Add a moonlit sandy beach and you have the best example of a picture being worth a thousand words. In years to come, that image would become a part of American pop culture.

In 1901, The Hawaiian Glee Club took four ukuleles on its tour of several big Mainland cities as part of its ten-piece, back-up band. In particular, the Glee Club played the Pan-American Exposition in Buffalo, New York. It wasn't until 1915, however, that the ukulele really hit big in the Mainland. This was the year that the Panama-Pacific International Exposition was held in San Francisco. In celebration of the completion of the Panama Canal, the Exposition offered Hawaii the opportunity to promote its products, land and people. With a $100,000 appropriation, the Hawaiian legislature approved the construction of the Hawaiian Building. One of the most popular attractions, the Hawaiian Building offered several shows a day featuring hulas and songs. The exposure of the ukulele during these shows gave many of the 17 million people who came to the Exposition a serious itch for the "jumping flea."

The Beginning of a Craze

One of the many performers at the exposition was Henry Kailimai, composer of "On The Beach At Waikiki." This song was important because it became one of the best known *hapa-haole* songs of the time. *Hapa-haole* (literal translation "half white") usually referred to someone who was of a mixed Hawaiian-Caucasian heritage. As a song, it meant that the lyrics were primarily in English, but with a few Hawaiian words thrown in (*hapa-haole* can also refer to a song where all the lyrics are in Hawaiian, the tune an original Hawaiian melody, but the arrangement is contemporized according to the prevailing sounds coming from the Mainland). Kailimai's song was also important because he played it on a ukulele.

Thanks to the powerful combination of the

allure of the islands, the hula dancers and Kailimai's performance, the Hawaiian craze was ignited, and the ukulele fad was born. Suddenly, it seemed that everyone wanted to play the uke. Music studios gave lessons, while department stores offered them for free with the purchase of a ukulele.

Immediately, Tin Pan Alley songwriters were writing dozens of Hawaiian novelty songs like "Hello, Hawaii, How are You?"; record companies were releasing a flood of Hawaiian records and several Mainland musical instrument makers began knocking out inexpensive ukuleles, barely keeping up with demand. The effort to sell Hawaii and its

culture was perhaps too successful. In some cases the Mainland makers were even identifying their ukes as "Made in Hawaii." This was particularly galling to the Hawaii Chamber Of Commerce, who had invested heavily to promote their own manufacturers.

Not all of the Mainland ukuleles were cheap imitations. As early as 1916, celebrated musical instrument makers such as C.F. Martin of Nazareth, Pennsylvania began making fine ukuleles. (More information on the great Hawaiian and Mainland manufacturers can be found in the third chapter).

The Hawaiian craze that flowed in the late teens began to ebb in the 1920s. However, the uke was firmly established as part of '20s music (see "Cliff Edwards" in chapter two). With the onset of big band music, interest in the uke began to wane by the thirties. The ukulele did enjoy a renaissance in the late '40s and early '50s. This was thanks, in part, to a new interest in Hawaiian music from the returning servicemen who had been based in the Pacific during World War II as well as the television omnipresence of baritone uke player Arthur Godfrey. At the same time, famous guitar designer Mario Maccaferri manufactured and sold over nine million plastic ukuleles. Amazingly, they had quite a nice tone and were easy to play. Despite the fact that so many were made, few turn up today. This is due probably to their being thought of as disposable "toys" in their time.

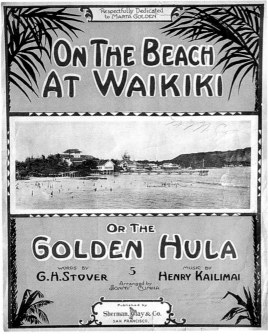

Souvenir program of the 1915 Panama-Pacific International Exposition in San Francisco, California.

—

The Royal Hawaiian Quartette playing at the Panama-Pacific International Exposition.

—

Sonny Cunha–The great *HAPA-HAOLE* singer and songwriter. Courtesy of Rick Cunha.

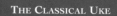

PANAMA-PACIFIC INTERNATIONAL EXPOSITION 1915 SOUVENIR GUIDE

NATURAL COLOR VIEWS, HALF TONES AND DESCRIPTIVE TEXT, PORTRAYING AND INTERPRETING THE EXPOSITION PALACES, COURTS, ART AND SYMBOLISM, WITH SUMMARY OF ATTRACTIONS ON THE ZONE.

THE CLASSICAL UKE

—

On February 13, 1927, the famous American composer Aaron Copland debuted his *Two Pieces For Violin And Piano*. The first piece, entitled "Nocturne," had a slow blues quality. The second, called "Ukelele [sic] Serenade," was marked *allegro vivo*, and was so-named because the arpeggiated chords in the right hand of the piano part were written to simulate the sound of a ukulele. Later in the piece the *pizzicato* violin plucking represents the uke.

Method To The Madness

In response to the Mainlander's desire to play the ukulele came a small forest of ukulele how-to-play books. In 1925, M. M. Cole of Chicago published the *5 Minute Guaranteed Ukulele Course*, followed in 1927 by Cole's *New Standard Ukelele Song Book* containing 200 songs with words. The price of each of these books was 25 cents. For 50 cents, Cole published *Wolff's Complete Ukulele Instruction Course* in 1928, including the new "photo-graphic" method showing hands forming chords and making strums on a "Le Domino" uke.

In 1925, May Singhi Breen and her husband Peter DeRose self-published the *Peter Pan Uke Method*. This and Breen's *New Ukulele Method*, published by the Robbins Music Corporation, were two of many Breen-created uke method books. Roy Smeck was another prolific uke songbook arranger. A few of his better known uke books include *New Original Ukulele Method* published by Alex H. Kolbe in 1928; the Smeck-arranged *Irving Berlin Songs*, published by the Irving Berlin Music Corporation in 1950; and Roy Smeck's *Ukulele Fun Book*, published in 1950 by the Edward J. Marks Corporation.

Year	Total
1915	12
1916	1,371
1917	1,988
1918	1,495
1919	3,541
1920	3,165
1921	1,669
1922	4,793
1923	4,785
1924	7,062
1925	10,870
1926	14,101
1927	5,860
1928	3,605
1929	3,349
1930	4,584
1931	2,718
1932	987
1933	737
1934	917
1935	985
1936	1,076
1937	1,436

MARTIN TABLE OF UKULELE PRODUCTION NUMBERS. COURTESY OF MARTIN GUITAR COMPANY.

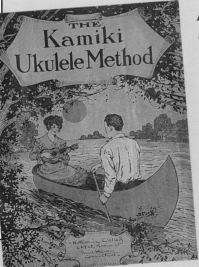

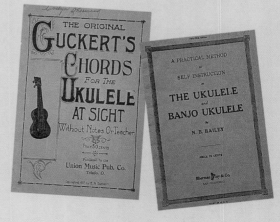

Here are a number of other better-known uke method/songbooks:

SELF INSTRUCTOR FOR THE UKULELE AND TARO-PATCH FIDDLE, 1912

by Major Kealakai, published by Southern California Music Company of Los Angeles. Major Kealakai was leader of the Royal Hawaiian Band from 1895 to 1896, "after the old throne" of Queen Lili'uokalani. Major Kealakai was an obvious booster of the uke, maintaining that "the ukulele is played by nearly everyone in Hawaii as well as the entire Pacific Coast. The harmony is there for the most difficult opera written if one would give it a complete and thorough study" and that anyone "can have more pleasure out of a ukulele than any other string instrument."

A PRACTICAL METHOD FOR SELF INSTRUCTION ON THE UKULELE AND BANJO UKULELE, 1914

by N.B. Bailey, published by Sherman, Clay & Company. A very early method book wherein the author states that "Unless accompanied by the Ukulele, the native Hula and Luau dances would be like meat without salt."

THE KAMIKI UKULELE METHOD, 1917

published by Wm. J. Smith & Co. This book featured a beautiful two-color illustration of a man and a woman in a canoe on the cover; he is paddling and she is strumming.

THE ORIGINAL GUCKERT'S CHORDS FOR THE UKULELE AT SIGHT (WITHOUT NOTES OR TEACHER), 1917

by E. N. Guckert, published by the Union Music Publishing Company. This book promises that "Nothing necessary to completeness has been omitted or has any useless matter been added to make this a large book."

SAM FOX MODERN METHOD FOR THE UKULELE AND BANJO UKULELE, 1919

by H. Kahanamo. Another very early method book.

ELITE METHOD FOR THE UKULELE, 1919

by Arling Shaeffer, published by Lyon and Healy. Large-size book featuring uke tablature and original songs by Mr. Shaeffer.

EZ METHOD FOR UKULELE AND UKULELE BANJO, 1924

Another Wm. J. Smith book that contains "just the necessary material for learning to play" the ukulele, tiple, uke-i-tar, guitar-uke and taro-patch.

SMITH'S COMIC SONGS FOR THE UKULELE, 1923

published by Wm. J. Smith Music Co. Inc. Featured many fractured songs and parodies written by Wm. J. Smith or in some cases Smill Bith. Includes "My Ukulele Queen."

Year	Total
1938	1,144
1939	862
1940	917
1941	1,443
1942	2,143
1943	8,163
1944	3,003
1945	2,495
1946	4,231
1947	1,567
1948	3,041
1949	8,076
1950	11,722
1951	6,214
1952	4,532
1953	4,901
1954	4,508
1955	3,848
1956	4,238
1957	3,900
1958	3,691
1959	5,356
1960	4,354
1961	5,126
1962	4,245
1963	4,319
1964	4,488
1965	2,801
1966	1,496
1967	1,425
1968	75
1969	111
1970	311
1971	512

The above totals are a combination of production figures and sales totals. Since the total sales and total manufactured are closely related, the above numbers are sufficient to establish Uke trends.

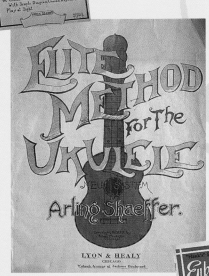

**"HANK'S" BOOK OF EUKADIDLES
FOR THE UKULELE, 1923**

by "Hank" Linet, published by Jack Mills
Inc. Two volumes of ukulele "ditties"
featuring the approved "Played-on-Sight"
Ukulele Chord System.

**MILLS SELF INSTRUCTOR
FOR THE UKULELE, 1924**

by C.E. Wheeler, published by Jack Mills
Inc. *Courtesy of Warner Bros. Publications.*

**PAUL SUMMERS INSTRUCTOR—
UKULELE AND GUITAR, 1932**

published by Paul Summers.
Includes the phone number
of Summers' studio in Honolulu.

**UKULELE IKE COLLECTION FOR
THE UKULELE, VOLUMES 1-3, 1949**

by Ukulele Ike (Cliff Edwards),
published by Robbins Music
Corporation. These three
songbooks (each with the
same cover in a different color,
in order—red, blue and green)
feature many big hits
of the day with uke
chord frames throughout.
*Courtesy of
Warner Bros. Publications.*

**FAMOUS COLLECTION FOR
THE UKULELE, ARRANGED BY
WENDELL HALL, 1950**

published by Famous Music.
This book introduced the reader to
"The Small Guitars of 1950,"
including the slightly-larger-than-
the-uke but smaller-than-
the-guitar Teeviola and Taraguitar.
*Courtesy of
Famous Music Corporation.*

**EVERYBODY'S FAVORITE
SONGS FOR UKULELE**

Courtesy of Music Sales Corporation.

LET'S PLAY THE UKE, 1959

by Harry Reser, published by MPH. One of
the best-selling "how-to" books of its day.

**MEL BAY'S
FUN WITH THE UKULELE, 1961**

by Mel Bay, published by Mel Bay
Publications. One of a multitude of
how-to books from one of the greatest
how-to companies.

UKULELE O HAWAII, 1973

by Ohta-San, published by Kamaka
Hawaii, Inc. A collaboration between
one of the greatest players of all time with
one of the greatest Hawaiian uke makers.
Courtesy of Kamaka Hawaii, Inc.

**HAPPY TIME UKULELE METHOD
AND SONG BOOK, 1987**

by Buddy Griffin, published by
Happy Time, Inc. According to
"Smiley," the book's mascot,
smiling while strumming
"it's just the natural thing to do!"

It's interesting to note that the publication of uke method and songbooks followed two distinct eras: The first occurring during the golden age of the teens and twenties, and then, again, the second right at the peak of Arthur Godfrey's popularity in the early 1950s. Also there were at least two attempts to sell a uke instruction course with a recording. One, by May Singhi Breen, was called *A Six-Minute Course on How to Play the Ukulele*, with Victor Record No.19740. Another, *R&M's Recorded Ukulele Course* by Jerry Oddo, was a record/book combo that promised to bring "the instructor into your home."

Other publishers who jumped on the uke-book bandwagon include Chas. H. Hansen with *Simplified Popular Song Hits for Ukulele*, and M. Witmark & Sons' *Great Themes for Ukulele—Hit Songs from Stage, Motion Pictures and TV*, arranged by Dan Fox and published in 1964.

The Uke and Tin Pan Alley

Tin Pan Alley songwriters in the 1915 to 1930s era, always looking to cater to as wide
an audience as possible, jumped head-first into the Hawaiian waters. Whether parodying the
Hawaiian language in "Oh, How She Could Yacki Hacki Wicki Wacki Woo" and "Yaaka Hula Hickey Dula,"
or getting laughs out of funny titles like "They're Wearing 'em Higher in Hawaii," the Tin Pan Alley
writers found Hawaii to be a fertile subject for songwriting.
Because the ukulele was synonymous with Hawaii, it is no surprise that the uke was often featured
in the lyrics of a lot of these songs and often rhymed with the words
"daily" and "gaily." Sometimes the uke even got top billing
in the song title. What follows are some uke-centered songs…

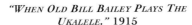

**"WHEN OLD BILL BAILEY PLAYS THE
UKALELE," 1915**
words and music by Chas. McCarron and
Nat Vincent. Includes the lyric "Bill Bailey
won his fame, with his old guitar, ukalele
is its name, in that land a far."

———

"MY WAIKIKI UKULELE GIRL," 1916
words by Jesse G. M. Glick; music by
Chris Smith. "Strum, strum, strum, on
your ukulele, pretty baby of the
Southern Sea." Ukulele/gaily rhyme.

———

**"I CAN HEAR THE UKULELES
CALLING ME," 1916**
words by Nat Vincent; music by
Herman Paley. One of the
most beautiful sheet music covers.

———

"THAT UKALELE BAND," 1916
words by Harry Edelheit and Sammy
Smith; music by Billy Vanderveer.
Note the spelling variation of ukulele.
Includes the lyric "That ukalele melody
is nice, the music seems
to come from Paradise."

**"WHEN THEY PLAY THE ROSARY
ON THE UKELELE," 1917**
words and music by Leonard Brown.
Brown (of Lowell, Massachusetts) is also
the publisher of this song; his promo lines
promise "songs with a punch."

———

"DREAMY PARADISE," 1920
words and music by Haven Gillespie,
Egbert van Alstyne and Erwin Schmidt.
From the collection of DeSoto Brown.

———

**"OH, HOW SHE COULD PLAY
A UKULELE," 1926**
words and music by Benny Davis
and Harry Akst.
Courtesy of Bourne Music.

OPPOSITE: DETAIL, *DREAMY PARADISE* FROM THE COLLECTION OF DESOTO BROWN

"SILENT UKULELE," **1942,**
words and music by Harry Owens.
Courtesy of Royal Music Publishing. From the
collection of DeSoto Brown.

———

"UNDER THE UKULELE TREE," **1926,**
words and music by Mort Dixon
and Ray Henderson.
Courtesy of Warner Bros. Music.
From the collection of DeSoto Brown.

———

"UKULELE LOU," **1924,**
words and music
by LeSoir, Dell and Casey.
Courtesy of Warner Bros. Music.
From the collection of DeSoto Brown.

———

"UKULELE LOU," **1924,**
words and music by Andrew Sterling.
From the collection of DeSoto Brown.

LOU

"MY HONOLULU UKULELE BABY," 1916,
words by Gerald N. Johnson
and music by Henry Kailimai.
From the collection of DeSoto Brown.

———

"UKELELE SWEETHEART," 1924,
words and music by Jack Murray,
Kenneth Stambaugh and Irving Mills.
Courtesy of Warner Bros. Publications.
From the collection of DeSoto Brown.

"HELLO, ALOHA!
HOW ARE YOU?," 1926,
words by L. Wolfe Gilbert;
music by Abel Baer.
This song features the lyric,
"Now I can uke and uke
and uke and uke
and you can uke a ukulele too!"
Courtesy of Warner Bros. Publications

SHED BY

RIS MUSIC CO.
NEW YORK

DETAIL RIGHT:
"HELLO, ALOHA! HOW ARE YOU?"

"SAY IT WITH A UKULELE," 1923
words and music by Art Conrad.
The uke is recommended as the
"proper thing to serenade a lady."
Courtesy of Shapiro Bernstein & Co., Inc.

———

"ON MY UKULELE," 1924
words and music by Mitchell Parish,
Mike Morris and Lou Herscher.
Ukulele/gaily rhyme.

———

"HUNIKA—A HAWAIIAN LULLABY," 1920
words and music by Fred Fisher
and Johnny S. Black.

———

"UKULELE BLUES," 1924
words and music by Claude Lapham,
May Singhi Breen and Samuel Kors.
Includes the lyric, "I bought a ukulele
and I strummed upon it daily."
Courtesy of E.B. Marks

———

"UKULELE LADY," 1925
words by Gus Kahn; music by Richard
Whiting. Perhaps the best-known song
with ukulele in the title.
Courtesy of Bourne Music.

———

*"GIVE ME A UKELELE
(AND A UKELELE BABY) AND
LEAVE THE REST TO ME,"* 1926
words and music by Lew Brown and Gene
Williams. Another daily/ukulele rhyme
as well as the line "with my little u-kin',
you kin leave the rest to me."
According to the sheet music cover,
the song was "England's Greatest Hit."
Courtesy of Shapiro Bernstein & Co.

"CRAZY WORDS CRAZY TUNE VO-DO-DE-O," 1927

crazy words by Jack Yellen; crazy music by Milton Ager (crazy uke arrangement by May Singhi Breen). The first verse starts out, "There's a guy I'd like to kill; if he doesn't stop I will, got a ukulele and a voice that's loud and shrill." Has a ukulele/daily rhyme.

Courtesy of Warner Bros. Music

"HUM AND STRUM, DO, DO, DO, THAT'S WHAT I DO," 1928

words by Billie Meyers; music by Elmer Schoebel. This song suggests that a little old friend (the uke) is just the thing to chase "lonesomeness away."

Courtesy of Forster Music

"MAKIN' LOVE UKULELE STYLE," 1949

words by Charlie Hayes; music by Paul Weirick. Recorded by Arthur Godfrey and Dean Martin.

Courtesy of Mayfair Music, a division of MPL Communications.

"THE UKULELE SONG," 1950

words and music by Terry Shand and Jason Matthews. Recorded by Arthur Godfrey on Columbia Records. From the collection of DeSoto Brown.

Courtesy of MCA Music.

Because the ukulele became a symbol for romance and a carefree life, some songs from this period used the uke simply as part of the cover illustration. Four delightful examples of this are…

"OH AGNES," **1919**

words by Arthur J. Jackson; music by Bud DeSylva. Tuxedoed gent with uke and a singing dog serenade the lovely Agnes on her balcony. DeSylva was also an accomplished uke player; his playing was featured on the first Jolson recording of "California, Here I Come," another DeSylva tune.

———

"TO BE IN LOVE," **1929**

words by Roy Turk; music by Fred E. Ahlert. Boy, girl, uke, moon.

Courtesy of Warner Bros. Music

———

"GOOD NIGHT MOON," **1931**

words and music by Walter Donaldson. Boy, girl, uke and moon.

Courtesy of Walter Donaldson Music

———

"ON A SUMMER HOLIDAY," **1942**

words and music by Carroll K. Cooper and Paul Learnard. Boy playing uke, girl, hayride.

Other pieces of sheet music featured a picture of the performer(s) of the song holding a uke. Sometimes these were songs associated with movies, especially, it seems, the films of Paramount Pictures. Examples of both include…

"WHEN MOTHER NATURE SINGS HER LULLABY," 1938 words and music by Larry Yoell and Glenn Brown. Great studio shot of Bing Crosby playing what looks like a fancy Hawaiian model. *Courtesy of Warner Bros. Music and the Estate of Bing Crosby*

"LOVE LETTERS IN THE SAND," 1931 words by Nick and Charles Kenny; music by J. Fred Coots. On the cover of the '50s version, Pat Boone with a vest and a baritone uke. *Courtesy of Bourne Music.*

"IN THE MIDDLE OF A KISS," 1935 words and music by Sam Coslow. Song from the Paramount picture, *College Scandal.* Cool photo/illustration of a coed character from the film strumming what looks like a Hawaiian uke. *Courtesy of Famous Music*

"IN A LITTLE HULA HEAVEN," 1937 words and music by Leo Robin and Ralph Rainger. Song from the Paramount picture *Waikiki Wedding.* Photo of Bing Crosby playing a taropatch uke seated next to island-happy Shirley Ross. *Courtesy of Famous Music and the Estate of Bing Crosby.*

"LET'S GET LOST," 1943 words by Frank Loesser; music by Jimmy McHugh. Song from the Paramount picture *Happy Go Lucky.* Neat shot of three of the stars holding ukes, including Mary Martin and Rudy Vallee. *Courtesy of Famous Music.*

"SONG FOR ANNA," 1972 original French words by Jean-Claude Massoulier, English words by H. E. R. Barnes; music by Andre Popp. Biggest hit for Ohta-San; recorded as an instrumental. *Courtesy of Warner/Chappell Music.*

RIGHT: DETAIL, BING CROSBY FROM *WHEN MOTHER NATURE SINGS HER LULLABY.*

Radio Waves

From 1935 to 1975, the legendary radio program *Hawaii Calls* sent the sounds of Hawaii (including a lot of uke strums) over the air to hundreds of stations throughout the Mainland and the world. Created by Webley Edwards with famed songwriter Harry ("Sweet Leilani") Owens as musical director, the very first program was beamed via shortwave to the West Coast on Saturday, July 3, 1935. Emanating literally from under the banyan tree in the courtyard of Oahu's Moana Hotel, *Hawaii Calls* was described as "Hawaiian music played by Hawaiians from Hawaii."

MEMORIES OF HAWAII CALLS—FROM THE COVER OF THEIR CD WITH THE ORIGINAL CAST. COURTESY OF DONALD "FLIP" McDIARMID III AND *HAWAII CALLS*.

The TV Pal

Thanks to Arthur Godfrey's huge popularity during the 1950s, millions of his television viewers were exposed to the ukulele. In fact, from April 4 to June 30, 1950, he actually gave ukulele lessons to his television audience on his show *Arthur Godfrey and His Ukulele*. This show ran on Tuesday and Friday nights from 7:45 to 8:00 and was sponsored by an orange juice concentrate that was partially owned by "The Redhead" himself. Godfrey, however, was by no means the only person to take the uke to the tube.

One of the largest television audiences in history gathered to watch Tiny Tim (with uke in hand) and Miss Vicky get married on *The Tonight Show*, December 17, 1969. Tiny made more than a dozen visits to *The Tonight Show* during his heyday, as well as regular appearances on *Rowan & Martin's Laugh In*, *The Merv Griffin Show*, *The Ed Sullivan Show*, and even the first episode of *Ironside*.

Also getting into the television act was Cliff "Ukulele Ike" Edwards who had his own short-lived show. Airing from May 23 to September 19, 1949, *The Cliff Edwards Show* was the remainder of the half hour that started with CBS's *Nightly News*. Edwards would tell stories, show off some of his huge collection of hats, sing some songs and, of course, play the ukulele.

In fact, it's a good bet that a uke was worked into most TV shows that were filmed in Hawaii or did an episode shot in Hawaii. This includes the *Brady Bunch* Hawaiian episode, and that most famous of comediennes playing the uke herself in a *Here's Lucy* episode called "Lucy Goes Hawaiian," originally broadcast February 22, 1971.

HARRY OWENS' SIGNATURE ROYAL HAWAIIAN UKE.

—

SONGBOOK FOR ARTHUR GODFREY UKE PLAYER.

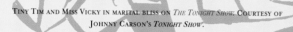

TINY TIM AND MISS VICKY IN MARITAL BLISS ON *THE TONIGHT SHOW*. COURTESY OF
JOHNNY CARSON'S *TONIGHT SHOW*.

—

LUCY AND LUCIE GOING HAWAIIAN. PERMISSION FOR THE IMAGE AND LIKENESS OF
LUCILLE BALL, COURTESY OF DESILU & CO., LLC.

T.V. PAL
UKE

U.S. PAT. NO.
2,597,154   2,614,448
MADE IN U.S.A.

THE UKE SHOWED UP ON *THE LAWRENCE WELK SHOW* IN SEVERAL VIGNETTES. LAWRENCE WELK WITH BARBARA BOYLAN AND BOBBY BURGESS ON *THE LAWRENCE WELK SHOW*. COURTESY OF THE WELK GROUP.

Poncie Ponce, one of the stars of the 1958 to 1963 TV detective show *Hawaiian Eye*, played the ukulele in his role as Kim, the cabdriver. A popular entertainer for years in Hawaii and the Mainland, Ponce was famous for performing "The Stars and Stripes Forever" on his Martin tenor uke with a custom-built, flip-up flag attached to the back.

PONCIE PONCE IN 1959.
COURTESY OF PONCIE PONCE.

BLUE HAWAII
ADVERTISING PHOTO.
COURTESY OF
THE ESTATE OF ELVIS PRESLEY.

—

THE ELVIS PRESLEY UKE

The Uke And Hollywood

In 1993, the ukulele played a small but crucial part in the hit movie, *In the Line of Fire*. As Clint Eastwood, playing a Presidential Secret Service agent, is racing to figure out what the word "skellum" means, another character happens to mention that the word "ukelele" is how he remembers a certain phone number. While Eastwood informs this guy that the correct spelling is u-k-u-l-e-l-e, he realizes that "skellum" might refer to a phone number.

The ukulele has been featured many times on the silver screen. Perhaps the uke's greatest starring role occurred in *Blue Hawaii* in the hands of the "King of Rock 'n' Roll" himself, Elvis Presley. A 1961 Paramount release, *Blue Hawaii* was Presley's biggest box-office hit and the soundtrack recording to the film (featuring Presley playing the uke on the cover) was his thirteenth Gold Record. The soundtrack recording was also Presley's longest-running Number One album on the *Billboard* charts, lasting a total of 20 weeks.

Another memorable movie role for the uke was in the hands of Marilyn Monroe in Billy Wilder's *Some Like It Hot* (1959, MGM). The uke is featured in the production number "Runnin' Wild." Among the special treats of the soundtrack recording of this movie are the famous Richard Avedon stills on the cover of Ms. Monroe cavorting with her uke.

Some other notable appearances of the uke occur in the following movies...

LAUREL AND HARDY, 1933
—
PENNIES FROM HEAVEN, 1981
USED BY PERMISSION
OF TURNER ENTERTAINMENT

PENNIES FROM HEAVEN, 1981

MGM/Turner Entertainment. Steve Martin plays a tenor uke during a performance of "Life Is Just a Bowl of Cherries." (The ukulele shows up in at least three Steve Martin movies, the other two being *Mixed Nuts* and *The Jerk*. The dubbed uke playing in The Jerk was provided by none other than Lyle Ritz! See Chapter 2 *The Great Players and Personalities*.) *Courtesy of Turner Entertainment.*

THE PURPLE ROSE OF CAIRO, 1985

Orion. Woody Allen gives the uke a supporting role in this wonderful movie. In front of a music store, Mia Farrow admits to Jeff Daniels that "I can play the ukulele. My father taught me before he ran away." Farrow then strums a very respectable "Alabamy Bound," on what looks like a Martin 0.

JOE VERSUS THE VOLCANO, 1990

Warner Bros. Tom Hanks really plays what looks like an early Martin 3M. While Hanks picks a bit in several scenes, in one scene he strums and sings "The Cowboy Song" while floating on his luggage in the middle of the ocean. Where better?

MIXED NUTS, 1994

Tristar. As one of the "nuts," Adam Sandler actually plays "Deck The Halls" on what appears to be a Martin 0.

SONS OF THE DESERT, 1933

Hal Roach. Ollie plays the uke and sings "Honolulu Baby" in this classic Laurel and Hardy misadventure.

A CONNECTICUT YANKEE IN KING ARTHUR'S COURT, 1949

Paramount. Bing Crosby teaches King Arthur's court musicians to swing. As he re-tunes one fellow's uke-like instrument, Crosby says, "There's a new tuning on these instruments, gonna sweep the country." After tuning up to the "my-dog-has-fleas" tuning, Crosby states, "There's a canoe that goes with these things, but that's another story."

HONOLULU, 1939

MGM. Gracie Allen has a couple of wonderful moments with a ukulele. In one scene she is shown having a hard time tuning her uke, finally admitting to her friend, "You see what's wrong, Dorothy...the dogs are all right, but the fleas are out of tune."

BUTCH CASSIDY AND THE SUNDANCE KID, 1969

Twentieth Century-Fox. Oscar-winning theme song, "Raindrops Keep Fallin' On My Head," features ukulele accompaniment.

The ukulele has played a role in a number of "island" movies by virtue of its presence in poster art, publicity stills or home video sleeves. Surprisingly, the uke doesn't always appear in the actual film.

For example, *Waikiki Wedding* (1939, Paramount) featured Bing Crosby in publicity stills with a uke. In the film, however, Crosby doesn't strum a note. The home video sleeve to the *Road to Singapore* (1940, Paramount), starring Bob Hope, Dorothy Lamour and Crosby, shows Hope strumming a uke that he never plays in the film. The same is also true for *Ma and Pa Kettle at Waikiki* (1955, Universal), where the poster shows Pa strumming while Ma hulas. In the movie, Ma does hula, but Pa is uke-less.

One interpretation of this phenomenon is that the ukulele was used in all of these situations as a symbol to suggest either "Hawaii" or "island," and "fun." Its actual use in the film was not nearly as important.

WAIKIKI WEDDING. WHILE CROSBY DOESN'T PLAY THE UKE, HE DOES SING "SWEET LEILANI," THE OSCAR-WINNING SONG WRITTEN BY HARRY OWENS. (THIS MOVIE PREMIERED IN HONOLULU ON MARCH 25, 1937 TO A PACKED CROWD, AND WAS PRECEDED BY A STAGE SHOW WITH POPULAR HAWAIIAN ENTERTAINER, RAY KINNEY, SINGING AND PLAYING HIS UKULELE.) COURTESY OF FAMOUS MUSIC CORPORATION AND THE ESTATE OF BING CROSBY.

MA AND PA KETTLE AT WAIKIKI. FROM A MOVIE POSTER ONE-SHEET. COPYRIGHT ©1997 BY UNIVERSAL CITY STUDIOS, INC. COURTESY OF MCA PUBLISHING RIGHTS, A DIVISION OF MCA INC. ALL RIGHTS RESERVED.

The Ukulele In Advertising

As one of the cultural ambassadors of Hawaii, as well as a symbol of fun and relaxation, the ukulele became a potent image for marketers. In the early years, Dole used colorful brands and labels on its canned pineapple. On the "Ukulele Brand"® label, Dole featured a lovely Hawaiian maiden strumming her uke.

In 1929, Lambert Pharmacal Co. of St. Louis used an illustration of a young woman playing the uke for its Listerine ad. Apparently, this "gay Philadelphia girl" was quite popular when strum- ming her uke outdoors. Inside, however, was a completely different story due to her "halitosis" (unpleasant breath). In the fifties, Tampax produced an ad with the image of a modern woman with her uke in order to evoke carefree confidence and grab the attention of the reader. Even as recently as 1994, the audio manufacturer Kenwood used an early picture of Tiny Tim with his uke in an attempt to apologize for the fact that even they couldn't make Tiny "sound good."

One of the most magnificent graphic depictions of the ukulele was created by Frank McIntosh. McIntosh, a California illustrator, was commissioned in the late thirties to design a series of menus for Matson cruise ships that regularly

Hawaii breaks all records for making life agreeable

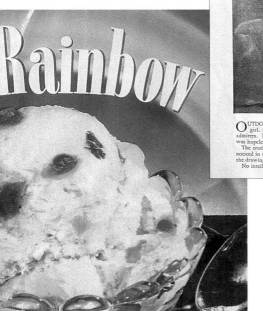

Outdoors adored ... indoors ignored

OUTDOORS they adored this gay Philadelphia girl. She was continually surrounded with admirers. But indoors it was another story. She was hopelessly out of things.

The truth is that her trouble which went unnoticed in the open, became instantly apparent in the drawing room.

No intelligent person dares to assume complete freedom from halitosis (unpleasant breath). Surveys show one person out of three is an occasional or habitual offender. This is due to the fact that odor-producing conditions (often caused by germs) arise constantly in even normal mouths.

The one way of keeping your breath always beyond suspicion is to rinse the mouth with full strength Listerine every morning and night and before meeting others.

Being a germicide capable of killing even the Staphylococcus Aureus (pus) germ in 15 seconds, Listerine first strikes at the cause of odors, and then, being a powerful deodorant, destroys the odors themselves.

No fastidious person should overlook this precaution. Lambert Pharmacal Co., St. Louis, Mo., U.S.A.

ALOHA

carried tourists to Hawaii. On the final night, the menu featured a multicolored illustration of a ukulele surrounded by an explosion of Hawaiian flowers and fruits. Diners were so taken with his designs that many saved the complete series of menus and had them framed in bamboo to hang in their homes. Today, these menus (complete and in good condition) are considered collectables and can fetch a high price. Another collectable uke-themed menu was designed by John Kelly for the Royal Hawaiian Hotel (see page 10).

The Ukulele Today

If you look carefully, there is plenty of evidence that the ukulele is very much alive and well today. The Ukulele Festival, held each year in Honolulu's Kapiolani Park, is just one example of the ukulele's continued vitality. Usually held on the last Sunday afternoon in July, the Ukulele Festival is the creation of Roy Sakuma. In 1996 this event celebrated its twenty-sixth anniversary and attracted four thousand ukulele players and fans. While the festival is one enormous recital for the hundreds of students in Roy Sakuma's ukulele school, the three-hour show also features many of the finest ukulele players in the world as well as current uke-playing Hawaiian pop stars. Appearing at these festivals are such luminaries as Ohta San, Lyle Ritz, Moe Keale, and Yuji Igarashi.

Further evidence comes from the year's worth of back orders for Kamaka ukuleles and the emergence of a number of luthiers (both in Hawaii and the Mainland), who are busy making fine ukuleles. Part of what is driving this renewed appreciation are con-

POSTER FROM THE '96 FESTIVAL

temporary Hawaiian artists who are also fine ukulele players. Performers like Troy Fernandez from the Ka'au Crater Boys, Willie K., Bryan Tolentino and Israel Kamakawiwo'ole are true ukulele virtuosos and have put this instrument front and center in their music. Many of these artists have performed at the Ukulele Festival in Kapiolani Park and they are musical heroes for the assembled. No better proof of the simple power of a uke and a voice was the line of children waiting to get Kamakawiwo'ole's autograph after his performance at the 1994 festival.

Another aspect of the uke revival in Hawaii is a renewed appreciation for all things Hawaiian, especially among the younger generations. As a big chapter in Hawaii's musical history, the ukulele is getting swept up in this enthusiasm. The ukulele also benefits from being a sophisticated instrument that is highly portable and relatively easy to learn. Whatever the reason, Roy Sakuma has seen a significant increase in the number of people who want to take uke lessons.

RIGHT: FLYING V
CENTER: ENIGMAPHON
LEFT: FLOUNDERLIN
THREE CONTEMPORARY UKES DESIGNED
AND MANUFACTURED BY BRIAN
STAPLETON.

—

BELOW: "KOA SOUP"
PHOTO BY PAUL SYPHERS

THESE ARE ENTITLED "TEN VIEWS OF THE UKULELE"—
spoofs on famous artists' works
BY JOHN BODEN. © PROF. JOHN BODEN, DIRECTOR OF
VISUAL ART, UNIVERSITY OF UKULELE STUDIES.
REPRODUCED BY PERMISSION OF THE
UKULELE ORCHESTRA OF GREAT BRITAIN.

Swagerty and Polk-a-lay-lee

In 1964, Ancil Swagerty hand built an oddly-shaped musical instrument that he thought might make an interesting piece of wall art. A friend wondered if it might be made to play, and the two of them worked on a model that could. The result of this was the three-sound-hole Treholipee, a 4 1/2-foot-long creature with a long neck and "paddle-shaped" tuners that played like a uke. Amazingly, it sounded better and played more easily than one would expect. From 1964 to 1967 Swagerty Specialties Company sold an estimated 60,000 Kooky-Ukes. Treholipees sold for $19.95, Kook-a-la-lees for $17.95 and Surf-a-leles for $13.95. Big national department stores such as Sears and the May Co. sold them, as did Southern California music stores. Steve Allen endorsed the Kooky-Ukes and a hang tag proclaimed "Steve Allen Presents The Kooky-Ukes...A New Sound For A New Generation." For pop culture archaeologists the Swagerty ukes also incorporated a cool Rick Griffin cartoon of a surfer shooting a curl and strumming his kooky uke.

On all of the promotional materials for Kooky-Ukes, Swagerty proudly listed his company's address as "Main Offices in Beautiful San Clemente (by the Sea), California." The ocean connection was important. For the beach, both the Treholipee and Kook-a-la-lee had an extra long end that could be stuck in the sand when not in use. The shorter Surf-a-lele was designed to be played while riding on a surfboard. Apparently, all the Kooky-Ukes were water resistant.

The similarly designed Polk-a-Lay-Lee was manufactured in Chicago by Peterson Products, also in the mid 1960s.

(Swagerty photos courtesy of Kitty Jones, Polk-a-lay-lee photo courtesy of John Nelson and Vintage Gear, Los Angeles, CA.)

Global Mania

The Ukulele Festival in Honolulu is not the only event of its kind. The island of Kauai and the town of Hayward, California, each boast its own festival. In 1990, an all day Ukulele Exposition was held in Montague, Massachusetts, and featured an exhibit, performance, lecture and a local radio tie-in. The producers of that expo are now continuing to put on even bigger events. Other known uke-enthusiast countries include Japan, the United Kingdom, and Canada, where the ukulele has, at times, been part of the school system.

Mainland ukulele clubs, where members get together on a regular basis to sing and strum, are on the rise. At last count, Southern California had at least three such clubs, with others known to exist in Chicago, Dallas, Santa Cruz and Connecticut. Part of this, no doubt, is driven by a nostalgia for the slower, simpler life portrayed in the old Tin Pan Alley songs. The uke, in this case, becomes an effective antidote to the frantic pace of life these days. On business trips, the uke can be a real "de-stresser," and, because of its small size, it can be carried on any plane.

The Collector Market

Another key part of the current ukulele story is the vitality of the collector market. Especially over the last ten years, interest in collecting vintage musical instru-

THE LAFFING UKE.
PHOTO COURTESY
OF PAUL SYPHERS

ments has exploded. While older acoustic and electric guitars, banjos and mandolins were the first to see their prices soar, vintage ukuleles have become highly sought after and collectable. This has been true particularly of the finer ukes, such as the old koa, brand name Hawaiian ukes, and the ukes made by Martin, Gibson, National and Lyon & Healy. It's not unusual for especially rare ukuleles to sell in the four and five figures. The cheaper, painted, "cartoony" ukes of the twenties and thirties have also become collector's items—even the plastic ukes of the fifties.

One of the world's biggest ukulele collections belonged to Akira Tsumura of Japan. His ukes have been on display at the Honolulu Academy of Arts and San Francisco International Airport.

Articles and books have been written about why people collect things. The current interest in collecting musical instruments, the Hawaiiana boom, and preserving artifacts of the twentieth century for succeeding generations somehow can't entirely explain away the passion of some uke collectors. Perhaps the best way to explain it is that you can't walk into a room full of ukes and not smile.

CHAPTER TWO

The First Players

Thanks to the playing of the earliest Portuguese players like João Fernandes and Augusto Dias, the machête began to attract attention and establish a potential market. This ultimately led to the refining of the machête into the modern-day ukulele.

The Great Players And Personalities

The contributions of these early players along with the encouragement and patronage of King Kalakaua were central to attracting other players, many of whom became virtuosos.

What follows are some of the best known players of the ukulele. Each one of them is a link in an ongoing chain that starts in 1879 and runs right through to today.

The Great Hawaiian Players

Ernest Kaai
(JANUARY 1, 1881–1962)

ERNEST KAAI was the first Hawaiian-born virtuoso ukulele player. Besides playing the uke, Kaai was a superb mandolin player and a talented violin, guitar and steel guitar player. He was equally as successful as a songwriter, arranger, singer, concert promoter, music teacher, and all-around impresario. Kaai was also the first to copyright music in Hawaii.

It was as a ukulele player, however, that Kaai really left his mark. According to the famous Hawaiian songwriter Johnny Noble ("My Little Grass Shack In Kealakekua, Hawaii"), Kaai was "Hawaii's greatest ukulele player." Due to his musical ability, he is credited for turning the ukulele into a featured instrument of the Hawaiian orchestra.

Kaai is also notable for publishing the very first ukulele instructional book: *The Ukulele, A Hawaiian Guitar and How To Play It* in 1906. His 1916 instructional, *The Ukulele, A Hawaiian Guitar*, presented the ukulele as a sophisticated musical instrument. Including the more exotic minor and diminished chords, the book describes in great detail how to produce a variety of complicated strums, especially the syncopated and ragtime strokes. Kaai gets quite

LEFT: KAAI'S *UKULELE SOLOS* SONGBOOK.
COURTESY OF DESOTO BROWN COLLECTION.

BELOW: ERNEST KAAI PLAYING THE UKULELE
WITH A FRIEND PLAYING
THE LAP STEEL, HONOLULU, CIRCA 1916.
PHOTO BY RAY JEROME BAKER,
THE BISHOP MUSEUM.

passionate about the instrument, admitting that "…any glee or musical club in the islands without the ukulele is far from being perfect" and that one could have "…more pleasure out of [an ukulele] in one month than on a guitar or any stringed instrument in one year."

Due to his efforts, by the 1920s the ukulele had become a permanent feature of Hawaiian ensembles. Around 1940, Kaai retired to Miami, Florida, where he opened a music store and continued to perform informally.

Jesse Kalima
(1920–1980)

JESSE KALIMA is recognized for presenting the ukulele as a solo instrument. At the age of 15, he entered the *Territorial Amateur Hour Contest* and won first place with his ukulele rendition of "Stars and Stripes Forever." This particular arrangement became a hit and a long career was established. Not only did "Stars and Stripes Forever" become Kalima's theme song, but for many years after it became an essential part of any aspiring uke player's repertoire.

Kalima's other ukulele contributions include being the first to use amplification and popularizing the larger-sized tenor uke. He preferred this size because of its greater resonance and wider fret spaces (for his stubby fingers). He is also credited with introducing the arrangement technique known as "chord soloing," where the melody and the harmony of a song are played simultaneously.

JESSE KALIMA
PLAYING HIS AMPLIFIED TENOR UKE.
—
JESS UKE—JESSE KALIMA, SOUNDS OF HAWAII.
FEATURES HAWAIIAN REPERTOIRE.

In 1938, with his two brothers and a cousin, Kalima formed a group called the Kalima Brothers. Some of the songs for which the Kalima Brothers were best known included Tin Pan Alley songs like "Jalousie," "Dark Eyes" and "Under The Double Eagle." All of them featured Jesse's unique brand of ukulele chord soloing. His recording career included "Dark Eyes" as a 78-rpm single and his first album called *Jess Uke*.

Eddie Kamae
(AUGUST 4, 1927)

EDDIE KAMAE was 14 years old when his brother Sam found a ukulele on a city bus. Not knowing the first thing about how to play it, yet in love with the sound, Kamae learned what he could from his brother, and then sought out any material or persons that could teach him more. At Charlie's Taxi, which also served as a musicians' hangout, in downtown Honolulu, Kamae met Shoi Ikemi. In 1948, the two teamed up to create the first all-ukulele group, the Ukulele Rascals.

For many years, the Ukulele Rascals played virtually every kind of music other than Hawaiian, including Latin, jazz, American folk, and popular songs. This was due to Kamae's desire for a musical challenge, finding the Hawaiian music too simple. With a background that included courses from the University of Hawaii in music theory, he even arranged and played very demanding classical pieces.

Like Jesse Kalima, Kamae also is credited with originating his own technique of "chord soloing," where, by plucking all four strings simultaneously, one can hear the melody and chords at the same time. Another Kamae trademark was a guitar-like *rasguea-do* sound achieved by quickly strumming his long fingernails across the strings. One popular song in the Rascals' repertoire that sparkles from this technique is their version of "Malagueña."

In 1957, Eddie Kamae had a major musical change of heart and dedicated himself to playing Hawaiian music only. Kamae started the Sons Of Hawaii in 1960 with the legendary slack key guitar player, Gabby Pahinui. With their unique blend of ancient and new Hawaiian musical elements, the Sons Of Hawaii revolutionized contemporary Hawaiian music.

THE SONS OF HAWAII IN 1980, EDDIE KAMAE IS SECOND FROM RIGHT.

THIS IS EDDIE KAMAE — *EDDIE KAMAE AND THE SONS OF HAWAII*, HULA RECORDS. A GOOD EXAMPLE OF KAMAE AFTER HE "DISCOVERED" HAWAIIAN MUSIC. FEATURED ARE FOUR TRADITIONAL HAWAIIAN MELODIES AND THREE SONGS WRITTEN BY QUEEN LILI'UOKALANI. THE LINER NOTES OBSERVE THAT KAMAE IS PARTICULARLY FOND OF THE QUEEN'S MUSIC BECAUSE HIS GRANDMOTHER WAS A COURT HULA DANCER DURING THE REIGN OF LILI'UOKALANI.

—

HEART OF THE UKULELE — *EDDIE KAMAE*, MAHALO RECORDS. A COMBINATION OF "BELOVED HAWAIIAN FAVORITES AND POPULAR INTERNATIONAL MELODIES." INCLUDES KAMAE'S UNIQUE RIGHT HAND WORK ON "GRANADA" AND "COME BACK TO SORRENTO." COURTESY OF LEHUA RECORDS.

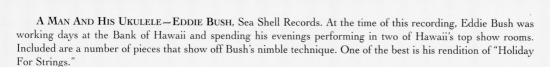

A MAN AND HIS UKULELE—EDDIE BUSH, Sea Shell Records. At the time of this recording, Eddie Bush was working days at the Bank of Hawaii and spending his evenings performing in two of Hawaii's top show rooms. Included are a number of pieces that show off Bush's nimble technique. One of the best is his rendition of "Holiday For Strings."

STRUM YOUR UKULELE—JOHN KAMEAALOHA ALMEIDA, 49th State Hawaii Record Co. Blind from the age of ten, Almeida was known as the "Dean of Hawaiian music." A very prolific composer of hundreds of melodies, the entire program of this album was written by Almeida. Almeida also served as the chief musician for the Matson Navigation Company from 1924–1927. As such, his job was to select the musicians who performed on the cruise ships that ran between Hawaii and the West Coast. Courtesy of Cord International/Hana Ola Records.

KING BENNIE NAWAHI—HOT HAWAIIAN GUITAR, 1928 to 1949, Yazoo Records. Born July 3rd, 1899 in Honolulu, "King" Bennie Nawahi became a prominent steel guitar, ukulele and mandolin player. In 1919, Nawahi got a job playing all three instruments with his older brother Joe's group, the Hawaiian Novelty Five, on the passenger ship Matsonia. Soon after, at the height of the "uke" craze, Nawahi left to pursue a solo career as a vaudeville singer and ukulele virtuoso. He astonished audiences by playing extremely difficult pieces on the uke, sometimes with only one hand or playing the uke behind his head. As a result, theater showman Sid Grauman crowned Nawahi "King of the Ukulele." Throughout an active recording career and even with the total loss of his eyesight in 1935, Nawahi played his uke. He passed away in Long Beach, California in 1985.

This album features 16 tracks of Nawahi playing mostly steel guitar and uke. Especially recommended is his original tune, "Ukulele Bennie." Courtesy of Yazoo Records.

NELSON WAIKIKI—UKULELE STYLIST, Tradewinds Records. A popular Hawaiian performer, Waikiki learned to play the uke at the age of ten. The liner notes point out that in addition to being a fine player, Waikiki "clowns" around when he plays, often strumming the uke from "above or behind his head." The album features a very delicate version of "Misty."

FAVORITE SELECTIONS BY JOHNNY UKULELE, Capitol Records. Born with the last name of Kaaihue, Johnny Ukulele was so-named during his long tenure as a regular on *The Harry Owens Show*. As the liner notes inform us: "Johnny Ukulele does not 'strum.' He plays...Under his fleet fingers the ukulele becomes a full-fledged instrument with a charming, distinctive sound." Courtesy of Capitol Records.

FACING FUTURE—ISRAEL KAMAKAWIWO'OLE, 1993, Bigboy Record Company. *Facing Future* has become one of the biggest-selling Hawaiian records of all time due especially to Kamakawiwo'ole's soulful recording of the medley "Over The Rainbow"/"What A Wonderful World." That particular recording has been heard in several major motion pictures and in TV dramas. Since his tragic death in 1997, he has become a legend in Hawaiian music and his beautiful voice and soft uke strumming can be heard everywhere in the Islands.

ON FIRE!—KA'AU CRATER BOYS, 1994, Roy Sakuma Productions. Features the red-hot ukulele playing of Troy Fernandez. Courtesy of Roy Sakuma.

While Eddie Kamae's legacy as a ukulele virtuoso is secure, he will also be remembered as the mentor and teacher of another virtuoso, Ohta-San.

Ohta-San
(HERB OHTA, OCTOBER 21, 1934)

As of this writing, the reigning ukulele virtuoso in the world is OHTA-SAN. Building upon the technique of his mentor, Eddie Kamae, Ohta-San has taken this simple four-string instrument into remarkable virtuosic terrain.

With encouragement from his mother, Herb Ohta began playing the ukulele when he was seven years old. He learned to play well enough that as a young boy in 1944 he won first prize playing the ukulele on Honolulu's *KGMB Radio's Amateur Hour*. Ohta was so good that after he won a second time, the judges decided he was too skilled to compete against the other contestants.

As a child, Ohta was introduced to a wide variety of music, including that of the great classical composers, as well as modern jazz. This was of particular value when the then-twelve-year-old Ohta met Eddie Kamae. In addition to teaching his young protégé a number of his techniques, Kamae encouraged Ohta to apply these approaches to his classical and jazz repertoire as well as the popular songs of the day. Ohta also studied music theory at the University of Hawaii.

While serving in the Marines from 1953 to 1963, Ohta had little time to play the ukulele. He did, however, make an appearance in 1955 on the *Ed Sullivan Show*. After the Marines, Ohta met with Don McDiarmid of Hula Records. It was McDiarmid who gave the then Herb Ohta his first break as a recording artist in 1964 and his professional name of Ohta-San. That first break, an original song called "Sushi," became a Number One hit in Hawaii and was later released by Warner Bros. Records.

Since 1964, Ohta-San has recorded over 70 albums for Decca Records, Warner Bros., Surfside, A&M and others, started a ukulele school, arranged ukulele songbooks, toured extensively throughout the world (he is especially popular in Japan) and played in many Waikiki hotels. He continues to record, tour and inspire new generations of players.

To hear him play is to experience someone who is an absolute master of his instrument. Playing mostly popular songs with only four strings at his command, he impresses you with both the marvelous clarity and precision of his playing as well as the innovative beauty of his arrangements.

SONG FOR ANNA—OHTA-SAN, A&M RECORDS. OHTA-SAN'S BIGGEST MAINSTREAM RECORDING, FEATURES THE HAUNTING HIT "SONG FOR ANNA." COURTESY OF POLYGRAM SPECIAL MARKETS.

—

RIGHT: OHTA-SAN WAITING TO GO ON STAGE AT THE 1996 UKULELE FESTIVAL IN WAIKIKI. PHOTOGRAPH BY ELIZABETH MAIHOCK BELOFF.

Another important aspect of Ohta's work is his songwriting. Over the years he has regularly put at least one or two of his own highly melodic tunes on his records.

UKULELE ISLE—OHTA-SAN, DECCA
RECORDS. OHTA-SAN'S DEBUT DECCA
RECORDING—TYPICALLY MASTERFUL PLAY-
ING BY ONE OF THE GREATEST UKULELE
VIRTUOSOS. FEATURES HAWAIIAN STAN-
DARDS AND CONTEMPORARY TUNES LIKE
"EBB TIDE." COURTESY OF MCA
SPECIAL MARKETS & PRODUCTS.

WHERE IS MY LOVE TONIGHT—OHTA-SAN,
1993, ROY SAKUMA PRODUCTIONS, INC.
OHTA-SAN EXHIBITS HIS CLASSIC "COOL
TOUCH" ON THIS COLLECTION OF
HAWAIIAN POP SONGS. STANDOUT TRACKS
INCLUDE "MY LITTLE GRASS SHACK IN
KALEAKAKUA" AND "MAKIN' LOVE
UKULELE STYLE." LYLE RITZ PUTS DOWN
HIS UKE TO PLAY BASS ON THIS ONE.
COURTESY OF ROY SAKUMA PRODUCTIONS.

*HOW ABOUT UKE? WIZARDS OF THE
UKULELE*—EDDIE KAMAE, OHTA-SAN,
JESSE KALIMA, EDDIE BUSH, LEHUA
RECORDS. A COLLECTION OF MOSTLY
HAWAIIAN REPERTOIRE PERFORMED INDI-
VIDUALLY BY FOUR GREAT UKE VIRTUOSI.
COURTESY OF LEHUA RECORDS.

PADDLIN' MADELIN' HOME

by Harry Woods

Introduced by
CLIFF EDWARDS
(UKELELE IKE)
in Mr.Chas. B. Dillingham's
Musical Comedy Success
"SUNNY"
at the
New Amsterdam Theatre
New York
MADE IN U.S.A.

Published by Shapiro, Bernstein & Co. MUSIC PUBLISHERS
Cor. Broadway & 47th Street
New York

CLIFF EDWARDS. COURTESY OF SHAPIRO,
BERNSTEIN & CO., INC.

CLIFF EDWARDS ("UKULELE IKE")
PHOTO COURTESY OF IAN WHITCOMB.

The Great Mainland and United Kingdom Players

Richard "Dick" Konter
(1882–1979)

RICHARD "DICK" KONTER was one of the volunteers on Commander Byrd's first expedition, May 9, 1926, to the North Pole. An American seaman, explorer and ukulele enthusiast, Konter was determined to introduce the ukulele to the Eskimos. With the help of the pilot, Konter smuggled a Martin koa uke aboard the plane. It was not until they reached Spitzbergen, the jumping-off point for the historic flight, that Konter realized that there were no Eskimos in that part of the world.

RICHARD KONTER WITH HIS UKE AT THE WHITE HOUSE. COURTESY OF MARTIN GUITAR COMPANY.

Despite this, the Konter uke entered the history books by being the first musical instrument to cross the North Pole. After the flight, everyone on the expedition, including Byrd, signed the ukulele. In addition, Konter was met in New York by twenty young women, who were former ukulele students, playing ukes in honor of his return. Later on, Konter gave the plain (but signed) little uke to the Martin Company and today it can be found in the Martin Museum in Nazareth, Pennsylvania. Konter, also known as "Ukulele Dick," was the author of a couple of method books called *Dick's Ukulele Method* and *Dick's Improved Ukulele Method*.

THE KONTER UKULELE THAT CROSSED THE NORTH POLE. COURTESY OF MARTIN GUITAR COMPANY.

Cliff Edwards
(JUNE 14, 1895–JULY 21, 1971)

CLIFF EDWARDS a/k/a UKULELE IKE was born in Hannibal, Missouri, and began his musical career performing in saloons around St. Louis. Because he couldn't always count on a piano being in the bar, Edwards learned to accompany himself on the ukulele. Prior to that, Edwards worked in a silent movie house, providing sound effects. Some of those "sounds" became part of his act, especially his ability to make sounds like a kazoo without actually playing one, a technique he called "eefin."

In 1918, Edwards formed a duo with pianist Bob Carleton, composer of the song "Ja-Da," a big novelty hit of the time. Largely on the strength of "Ja-Da," Edwards and Carleton got some good bookings on the vaudeville circuit. When Carleton left the duo to concentrate on songwriting, Edwards teamed up with stuttering comedian/pianist Joe Frisco. According to legend, they were performing in Chicago when a waiter, who could never remember Edwards' first name, started referring to Cliff as "Ike." The "Ukulele" part, of course, was

UKULELE IKE
SINGS AGAIN —
CLIFF EDWARDS,
Disneyland Records.
The third album released on
the Disneyland label, this
record followed closely on the
heels of the Pinocchio
soundtrack, which, of course,
featured Edwards as
"Jiminy Cricket." Given
Edwards' new publicity lift
at the time, Disneyland
re-recorded 16 songs that
had been Ukulele Ike hits
in the twenties, including
"Singin' in the Rain,"
"June Night," "Ja-Da,"
and "I Cried for You."
The liner notes point out
that the number "37"
was Edwards' lucky number
(he was the 37th person to
test for the voice of
Jiminy Cricket).

an obvious addition.

Becoming one of the great singing stars of the 1920s, Edwards found fame on both stage and screen. On the stage side, in 1924, he strummed and sang the song "Fascinating Rhythm" in Gershwin's *Lady Be Good* starring F r e d a n d A d e l e Astaire. At the end of the twenties, he headed to Hollywood to pursue a movie career. One of his greatest claims to fame was that he introduced the song "Singin' in the Rain" in the movie *Hollywood Revue of 1929.*

In addition to a number of theatrical credits and over 100 movie appearances, Edwards also made hundreds of recordings and sold millions of records (Larry Kiner's biography of Edwards reports sales of "74 million recordings"), remarkable for any time. Between the years of 1922 to 1936, Cliff recorded for many different labels including Columbia and Pathé-Perfect. He had a string of hits between 1924 and 1933 with "It Had To Be You," "If You Knew Susie (Like I Know Susie)," "Paddlin' Madelin' Home," and "I Can't Give You Anything But Love." In addition to Edwards' beautiful singing voice and unique scat singing, many of these records feature his uke playing.

While Edwards' uke playing was meant primarily to serve his voice, he was actually a fine player. (Listening to some of the compilations of his recordings as well as seeing pictures of him, it appears that he particularly liked to play the tenor uke.) Thanks to his records, live performances and broadcasts, Edwards played a major role in the popularization of the ukulele in the twenties. As a result, much of the sheet music from that period included ukulele chord diagrams. He also put out three collections of standards arranged for the uke.

In 1940 Edwards had his biggest success when he was cast as the voice of Jiminy Cricket in Walt Disney's *Pinocchio*. Walt Disney himself decided that Edwards' voice, "the voice with the smile," would be perfect for the role. While few people today know the name of the person singing "When You Wish Upon A Star," everyone knows that voice.

Wendell Hall
(AUGUST 23, 1896–APRIL 2, 1969)

It wasn't until WENDELL HALL was in his late twenties that he started to play the ukulele. While Hall had learned to play a number of other musical instruments, it was the uke that he used to back up his performance on what would become his biggest hit. On November 16, 1923, Hall released "It Ain't Gonna Rain No Mo'," on Victor records. Based on an old country folk tune, Hall provided new lyrics to "It Ain't Gonna Rain No Mo'," and his version became Victor's biggest hit of the year, selling over two million copies.

Also known as "The Red-Headed Music Maker," Wendell Hall made other contributions to the uke world, including a number of songbooks, such as his *Famous Collection for the Ukulele,* published in 1950 by the Famous Music Corp. He also had his own Wendell Hall-signature ukulele known as the "Redhead." Like Cliff Edwards, Hall had a career that spanned vaudeville, radio, television, world tours and the movies.

"IT AIN'T GONNA RAIN NO MO'."
COURTESY OF FORSTER MUSIC.

Johnny Marvin
(JULY 11, 1897–DECEMBER 20, 1944)

JOHNNY MARVIN was one of the top recording artists of the twenties. Born in a covered wagon, Johnny Marvin's birthplace was probably somewhere in between Missouri and Butler, Oklahoma, where his family finally settled.

The Marvins were quite a musical family. Marvin's dad played the fiddle and the guitar, while his mother played the concertina and sang. Arguments with his father over the small amount of money they would earn playing neighborhood dances led Marvin to leave home repeatedly through his teenage years. In

1915 while still in his teens, Marvin joined a troupe of Hawaiian performers called the "Royal Hawaiians," filling in for an older member who had died on the tour. Marvin colored his hair black, stained his face, learned to speak pidgin Hawaiian and, most importantly, learned to play the ukulele.

Between 1917 and the mid twenties, Marvin served in the Navy, worked as a barber in San Francisco, put together a vaudeville act and married. In 1924, Marvin made his first record, which was followed by dozens more throughout the rest of the twenties. At the time Marvin imitated Ukulele Ike, who was very popular then, and even recorded under the name of Honey Duke and His Uke. Marvin appeared in a Broadway musical called *Honeymoon Lane* in 1926, which included a song he later recorded, entitled "Half a Moon."

With his recording career in full bloom, Marvin next teamed up with his brother Frankie as a vaudeville act. The show included Johnny performing some of the songs that had made him famous, while Frankie played the comedian.

When the Depression hit, Marvin's career moved to the new world of radio where he became known as "The Lonesome Singer of the Air." In the mid thirties, Marvin moved out to Hollywood to work with his friend "The Singing Cowboy," Gene Autry. While Marvin had written songs in the past including "Thinking of You, Thinking of Me," and his signature song "At The Close of a Long, Long, Day," he went on to compose

JOHNNY MARVIN UKE.
—
JOHNNY MARVIN: A VOICE OF THE '20s, TAKE TWO RECORDS. THIS 1987 COMPILATION FEATURES MOSTLY LESSER-KNOWN NOVELTY SONGS THAT MARVIN RECORDED. MARVIN'S "12TH STREET RAG" SHOWCASES HIS UKULELE SKILLS. ALSO RECOMMENDED IS THE DELIGHTFUL "HALF A MOON."

ROY SMECK "VITA UKE."

around 80 songs for Autry films, the best known being "Goodbye Little Darlin'."

Another contribution Marvin made to the ukulele was his signature uke made by the Harmony Company. This uke is notable for its unique airplane-shaped bridge. While he was on tour in England in 1928, Marvin presented a special version of this uke (with gold-plated trimmings) to King Edward VIII.

Roy Smeck
(1900–APRIL 5, 1994)

Known as the "Wizard of the Strings," ROY SMECK played a number of musical instruments brilliantly, including the guitar, banjo and the lap steel guitar. As astonishing as he was with all of those instruments, Roy was most wizard-like on the ukulele.

Born in Reading, Pennsylvania, Smeck moved with his family to Binghamton, New York when he was fourteen years old. His first musical instruments were the Jew's harp, harmonica and the (very popular at the time) Autoharp. Originally taught by an uncle, Smeck rigged up a shoulder device so that he could play the harmonica and the Autoharp simultaneously. It was Smeck's father who showed him how to play three chords on an old Stella guitar and, in doing so, launched a career.

According to Smeck in an interview with *Guitar Player* magazine, "If my father hadn't played those three chords, I wouldn't be here today."

Early on, Smeck developed an almost obsessive relationship with his musical instruments. By age fifteen, he had quit school, was working in a shoe factory and playing guitar, banjo and ukulele whenever and wherever he could. Later he was fired from the shoe factory for his habit of taking his uke to work with him and playing it in the men's room. In a true display of over-the-top passion Smeck admitted in one interview, "I even took it [the uke] to bed with me."

Smeck's big break occurred while he was working in a Binghamton music store. A salesman for a wholesale musical instrument house caught him running through his highly disciplined practice routine while on a break. Impressed by what he heard, he invited agents for the RKO Vaudeville Circuit to hear Smeck play. In 1926, after a successful audition in the Hamilton

Theatre in New York City, Smeck was hired for 26 weeks to play the RKO circuit at $250 per week.

Smeck's stage routine included a demonstration of his abilities on several stringed instruments. After showing his prowess on banjo and Hawaiian guitar, Smeck would finish with the ukulele and perform "The 12th Street Rag" and a medley that included "Five Foot Two," "Ain't She Sweet" and "The Stars and Stripes Forever."

While Harry Reser was Smeck's major influence when it came to the banjo, it was Johnny Marvin who influenced Smeck's ukulele playing. It was Marvin's version of "The 12th Street Rag" that inspired Smeck to not only improve upon Marvin's rendition, but to push the ukulele further as a solo instrument. He applied some of the tricks he learned on the banjo to the ukulele, which included complex strums that made it sound like not one, but two or three ukes being played. Imitating a tap dance break, Smeck would also tap on the body of the uke with his fingers.

Other "Smeckisms" included playing the uke like a violin and playing it upside down, blowing in the soundhole like someone would on a soda bottle, spinning the uke, imitating a train, strumming the uke off his knee and swinging it in such a way that he would create a vibrato sound. One big show stopper was a uke-harmonica duet— holding the harmonica in his mouth without a brace!

While known initially on the vaudeville circuit, Smeck eventually wound up with his own five-day-a-week radio show on WOR in New York, where he gave his listeners a 15 minute lesson on a different musical instrument each day. He performed on all the major TV variety shows (Jack Paar's, Ed Sullivan's, Steve Allen's) and even made a number of short films for some of the Hollywood studios. One of these short films, *Farewell Blues*, made for Paramount in the late forties, was the first to show a multi-tracked Smeck playing the guitar, lap steel, banjo and ukulele simultaneously.

At the height of his popularity, Smeck was in demand as a session player (for artists like Gene Autry) and made dozens of his own recordings. Two notable recordings that featured Smeck's ukulele playing are *The Magic Ukulele of Roy Smeck*, ABC-Paramount, and *Roy Smeck and His Magic Uke*, Kapp. Both are hard to find, but absolutely essential for any good uke record collection. He also published over thirty ukulele instruction books and songbooks.

One of Smeck's greatest ongoing legacies is the many lines of musical instruments produced under his name. The Harmony Company in Chicago manufactured and sold millions of Smeck ukes. In particular, the pear-shaped Vita Uke with the seal cutout soundholes is a great "player" and quite collectable (page 61).

A 1982 documentary about Smeck's life entitled *The Wizard of the Strings* was nominated for an Academy Award. Throughout much of his later years, Smeck continued to teach and perform. On Friday, April 8, 1994, he passed away at 94.

THE MAGIC UKULELE OF ROY SMECK, ABC-PARAMOUNT. THIS IS THE FIRST SMECK UKE RECORD AND FEATURES HIS FAMOUS "12TH STREET RAG" SOLO. LIKE MANY OF THE OTHER VIRTUOSI, SMECK PROMOTES THE NOTION THAT THE UKE, GIVEN ENOUGH PRACTICE, CAN BE A "SOLO INSTRUMENT." IN THE LINER NOTES HE WROTE, "MY SLOGAN HAS ALWAYS BEEN, 'YOU CAN PLAY SOLOS ON THE UKE.'" FEATURED ON THE RECORD IS THE SMECK-COMPOSED SONG "UKE SAID IT." COURTESY OF MCA SPECIAL MARKETS & PRODUCTS.

ROY SMECK AND HIS MAGIC UKE, KAPP RECORDS. THIS EXTRAORDINARY RELEASE ALSO FEATURES THE FAMOUS GUITARIST BUCKY PIZZARELLI. IN ADDITION, IT INCLUDES TWO SMECK ORIGINALS, "MAGIC UKULELE WALTZ" AND "ROCKIN' THE UKE." COURTESY OF MCA SPECIAL MARKETS & PRODUCTS.

BELOW: ROY SMECK CONCERT UKE

May Singhi Breen
(D. DECEMBER 19, 1970)

Also known as "The Ukulele Lady," MAY SINGHI BREEN devoted much of her life toward the recognition of the ukulele as a legitimate musical instrument. Breen played a key role in establishing that recognition with the Musician's Union. Her career was sparked in 1922 when she received a ukulele as a Christmas gift. Because she didn't know how to play the uke, she tried to exchange it for a bathrobe at the department store where it was purchased. When this proved unsuccessful, she decided to take uke lessons.

Obviously, Breen was a big believer in the uke as a solo instrument. In her method book

entitled *May Singhi Breen New Ukulele Method for Beginners and Advanced Students* (Robbins Music Corp.), she promotes the concept of chord soloing with her slogan "UKE CAN PLAY THE MELODY."

Breen and her husband, songwriter Peter DeRose ("Deep Purple," "Just Say Aloha") appeared on the radio (NBC and WJZ) for 16 years as *The Sweethearts of the Air*. She was also a successful songwriter and arranger; many pieces of sheet music include the credit of "ukulele arrangement by May Singhi Breen." In her bid to show how far the uke could be taken, she wrote a 16-minute rhapsody for uke and performed it at the Aeolian Hall in New York with the Paul Whiteman Orchestra.

A passionate teacher of the ukulele (she had her studio and company, Uke Trades Publishing Co., at 16 W. 72nd St. in New York City), Breen was a booster of forming ukulele-oriented clubs. In her *New Ukulele Method*, she writes: "It [the uke] should head the list of every recreational program in schools, camps and Girls' and Boys' Clubs in educational centers. Group-playing leads to enjoyment for young and old. Form clubs—play in groups—and watch the progress. I wish I could tell you of the many lasting relationships that have resulted through the medium of the groups, which I had the pleasure of forming and training."

COURTESY OF THE ESTATE OF MAY SINGHI BREEN DEROSE.

Arthur Godfrey
(AUGUST 31, 1903–MARCH 16, 1983)

For three months in 1950, ARTHUR GODFREY had a short-lived television show called *Arthur Godfrey and His Ukulele* where he actually gave uke lessons to his television audience. While that show may not have been a big hit, at the beginning of 1949 Godfrey was the first performer in television history to have two top-rated TV shows running simultaneously — *Arthur Godfrey's Talent Scouts* and *Arthur Godfrey and His Friends*. At his peak popularity in the early 1950s, his nine radio and television shows were enjoyed by 40 million fans per week and contributed an astonishing 10 million dollars a year in advertising, or about 12% of CBS's total annual advertising revenue. No wonder it was said that Godfrey was the most valuable single property of the Columbia Broadcasting System — even more valuable than its president or board of directors.

Godfrey learned to play the ukulele in the early twenties from a Hawaiian shipmate while in the Navy at Great Lakes Training Station. As early as 1929, he was giving uke lessons on the radio in Baltimore. It was in January 1950 that he made an impulsive decision to promote his favorite musical instrument on his radio and TV shows. Every week, Godfrey would enter the nation's living rooms dressed in his Hawaiian shirt, strumming a ukulele and singing songs like "Makin' Love Ukulele Style."

In addition, one of his regulars on *...Friends* was Hawaiian singer and uke player Haleloke. Godfrey was a true bridge between the first wave of the uke and what was to be his self-created craze.

As a result of this priceless exposure, the ukulele experienced a major revival in the fifties. Godfrey endorsed the famous plastic Maccaferri "Islander" ukulele and helped to sell nine million of them at $5.95 each. Since 1929, uke sales had been running about 5000 units a year; when Godfrey gave his

JAZZ FOR THE PEOPLE—ARTHUR GODFREY & HIS FRIENDS, SIGNATURE. THIS DELIGHTFUL RECORD FEATURES GODFREY HAVING A PARTICULARLY GOOD TIME SINGING AND SWINGIN' HIS WAY THROUGH A GROUP OF STANDARDS. ESPECIALLY NOTABLE IS GODFREY'S "JAZZY" BARITONE UKULELE PLAYING THROUGHOUT.

—

VEGA "ARTHUR GODFREY" BARITONE UKE.

This box contains 16 page Song Book and

Arthur Godfrey

UKE PLAYER*

Snap it on . . .

**PLAY LIKE A "PRO"
WITHOUT LESSONS**

"blessing" on the uke, 5000 ukes were sold in a few days. It was determined that his six months of uke enthusiasm on his nine weekly shows resulted in sales of 1,700,000 instruments. In her *New Ukulele Method*, May Singhi Breen writes that "...thanks to the one and only Arthur Godfrey, the ukulele is now called 'the family instrument of America.'" Godfrey's message was hard to ignore: "If a kid has a uke in his hand, he's not going to get in much trouble."

In addition to his broadcasts, recordings and live performances with his uke, Godfrey made one other key contribution to the ukulele: It was Godfrey who asked Eddie Connors to design what later became the baritone ukulele.

George Formby
(MAY 26, 1904–MARCH 6, 1961)

Born in Lancashire, England, GEORGE HOY BOOTH was the son of a successful Edwardian music hall comedian whose stage name was George Formby. When the elder Formby died in 1921, the younger George decided to take over his father's act. In a backstage dressing room eighteen months later, Booth met a fellow performer strumming a banjulele. A cross between a banjo and a uke, the banjulele plays like a uke but sounds like a banjo.

In need of money, the owner sold it to Booth, who immediately began to teach himself how to play. (Booth was also intrigued by the instrument due to Cliff "Ukulele Ike" Edwards who was popular at this time.) On a bet from his fellow entertainers that he didn't have the nerve to put the banjulele in his

act, Booth performed with it at the Alhambra Theatre in Barnsley, England and brought the house down. In this instrument, Booth found what was to become one of the two crucial partners in his career. Soon after, he felt confident enough to take on his father's stage name and he became the second GEORGE FORMBY.

The other key to Formby's career was Beryl Ingham, a dancer. It was after they married that his career really took off. Under her watchful eye, Formby became one of the most popular and highly paid entertainers in England. In addition to his live act, Formby appeared with his banjulele in twenty-two hit movies. The key to his charm was that he reminded the public of the boy next door—lacking in sex appeal, but very funny. His was a "smile of perpetual wonder at the joyous incomprehensibility of the universe."

As a self-taught player, Formby had his own unique syncopated strumming that still remains difficult to duplicate. He also was famous for hits like "Leaning on a Lamp Post" and naughtier songs like "With My Little Ukulele in My Hand."

GEORGE FORMBY
COURTESY OF DECCA RECORDS.

THE KEECH "BANJULELE" BANJO.

The Banjulele

In the mid 'teens there was a growing interest in making the ukulele louder and sturdier. In 1925, Hawaiian native Alvin Keech applied for a U.S. trademark for the banjulele, a ukulele and banjo hybrid. Keech banjuleles received promotional help from Alvin's "ukulele soloist" brother, Kelvin, and were manufactured in Los Angeles and England. The concept proved very popular and companies such as Gibson, Ludwig and Harmony designed and manufactured their own banjo-ukes. These instruments were tuned like ukes and used regular ukulele strings.

Lyle Ritz
(JANUARY 10, 1930)

With three albums of jazz ukulele, LYLE RITZ has secured his place in uke history. The first two of these remarkable records, *How About Uke?* and *50th State Jazz*, were released on Verve Records in the fifties, demonstrating brilliantly how far this simple four-stringed instrument could be taken.

Playing a tenor ukulele tuned down to guitar tuning with the top string up an octave in the traditional "my dog has fleas" tuning, Ritz (with well-known studio musicians on horns, flute, bass and drums) tackles some of the most challenging jazz standard tunes like "Moonlight In Vermont," "Don't Get Around Much Anymore," and "Lulu's Back In Town." As the liner notes on *How About Uke?* inform us: "No quarter is asked; Lyle meets jazz on its own ground, and the tricks usually associated and heard with a novel instrument are conspicuously absent."

Part of his musical fearlessness on the uke may be that Ritz did not come to the uke by way of the guitar or other fretted instruments. As a boy growing up in Pittsburgh, he studied violin for ten years.

It was as a salesman at the Southern California Music Company in downtown Los Angeles that he discovered the ukulele. Part of his job was the demonstration and sale of miscellaneous instruments. Thanks once again to Arthur Godfrey, Ritz was demonstrating a lot of ukes. Gravitating to a Gibson tenor, he became more and more enamored with the instrument. (The uke that is pictured on his two Verve recordings is a Gibson tenor that was specially "cutaway" to allow for high-up fretwork.) Today, he will tell you that it was the "sound" of the tenor uke that first captivated him, and that it was "my size instrument."

Despite a brief flirtation with the guitar and even the tuba and trumpet, Ritz became known for a much larger instrument—string bass. As an A-list studio string bass player in the sixties and seventies, he contributed to some 5,000 recordings, including "Good Vibrations," "You've Lost That Lovin' Feeling" and "I've Got You Babe." Now, as a resident of Hawaii, Ritz is still playing bass and ukulele, arranging uke songbooks and making recordings.

50TH STATE JAZZ—LYLE RITZ AND HIS JAZZ UKULELE, 1959, VERVE RECORDS. THIS RECORD HAS MORE OF A HAWAIIAN THEME WITH SONGS LIKE "BLUE HAWAII" AND "ON THE BEACH AT WAIKIKI." THE UKE PLAYING IS, OF COURSE, JAW DROPPING AND THE OTHER PLAYERS ARE EQUALLY FINE. COURTESY OF VERVE RECORDS.

—

HOW ABOUT UKE?—LYLE RITZ PLAYS JAZZ UKULELE, 1958, VERVE RECORDS. THE FIRST OF TWO JAZZ UKE ALBUMS RITZ CUT FOR VERVE. RITZ TAKES THE UKE INTO UNCHARTED TERRITORY WITH REMARKABLY SOPHISTICATED CHORDAL MOVEMENT AND INSPIRED SINGLE-NOTE SOLOS. THE RECORD INCLUDES STANDARDS LIKE "DON'T GET AROUND MUCH ANYMORE," "TANGERINE," AND "HOW ABOUT YOU," AS WELL AS AN ORIGINAL, "RITZ CRACKER." COURTESY OF VERVE RECORDS.

—

LYLE RITZ/TIME…UKULELE JAZZ WITH BASS, DRUMS &PERCUSSION, 1995, ROY SAKUMA PRODUCTIONS, INC. THIS RECORDING IS AN ANSWERED PRAYER FOR RITZ FANS. FEATURED ARE RE-RECORDINGS OF SOME OF THE STANDARDS HE CUT WITH HIS VERVE RECORDS ("LULU'S BACK IN TOWN," "BLUE HAWAII," "LITTLE GIRL BLUE," "I'M BEGINNING TO SEE THE LIGHT"), PLUS SOME NEW TUNES LIKE BILLY JOEL'S "JUST THE WAY YOU ARE" AND THE DELIGHTFUL RITZ-PENNED "TIME HAS DONE A FUNNY THING TO ME." COURTESY OF ROY SAKUMA PRODUCTIONS.

In 1994, Ritz and Ohta-San were playing their ukes together on tour and in the studio, and in November of 1995, Ritz released a uke recording entitled *Lyle Ritz/Time….* No doubt what drives Ritz today is the same thing that drove him to make his two legendary records: "…to find out what can be accomplished with the ukulele in jazz and to give the instrument real stature in contemporary music of serious nature" (liner notes on *50th State Jazz*).

Tiny Tim
(APRIL 12, 1933–NOVEMBER 30, 1996)

TINY TIM was born Herbert Khaury in Manhattan's Park East Hospital. He was more closely associated with the ukulele than anyone else in the world. His mother, Tillie, came from an orthodox Jewish family, and his father, Butros Khaury, was a Lebanese textile worker. Young Herbert Khaury grew up in Washington Heights, New York.

TINY TIM
COURTESY OF ROUNDER RECORDS

Tiny Tim's fascination with the ukulele was inspired by another great "uke" personality— Arthur Godfrey. In the Tiny Tim biography by Harry Stein, Tiny admits that "it was because Mr. Godfrey played the ukulele that I began to play myself." Tiny goes on to say that he learned the chords from a book Godfrey wrote with Don Ball called *You Too Can Play The Ukulele*. One of his first ukes was an "Arthur Godfrey" plastic uke that he bought for six dollars. (Tiny Tim didn't meet Arthur Godfrey until 1968, where at a roast for Walter Cronkite, Godfrey said to him, "So, we finally meet.")

Early on, Tiny Tim applied his knowledge of the uke to learn to play the tenor guitar, an instrument that was far more mainstream for the time. However, he went back to the ukulele because it was easier to travel with, especially as he got thrown out of one audition after another. In fact, it's because Tiny was "booted out" of these auditions so quickly that he began his tradition of carrying his uke in a shopping bag (rather than a case) for a fast exit.

Considering the large physical presence of "Tiny" Tim, his long hair, and his unusual falsetto voice, the ukulele somehow completed the picture in a comical way. Tiny's repertoire was made up mostly of turn-of-the-century and Tin Pan Alley songs, which were exceptionally well-served by uke accompaniment.

After struggling for years in Greenwich Village clubs, Tiny attracted the attention of Reprise Records. In 1968, he cut his first album, *God Bless Tiny Tim*,

FOREGROUND: UKULELE ONCE OWNED BY TINY TIM, NOW IN AUTHOR'S COLLECTION

CENTER RIGHT: DETAIL FROM *GOD BLESS TINY TIM*—TINY TIM, REPRISE RECORDS. TINY'S FIRST AND BIGGEST ALBUM. FEATURING HIS HIT VERSION OF "TIP-TOE THRU' THE TULIPS WITH ME," FALSETTO, UKE-STRUMMING AND ALL. THIS ALBUM IS TRULY AN ORIGINAL. PRODUCED BY THE FAMED ROCK PRODUCER RICHARD PERRY.

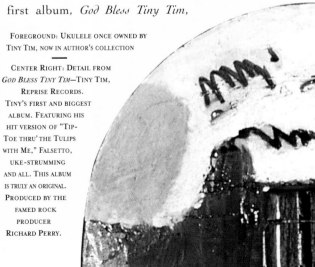

which featured the huge hit "Tiptoe Thru' the Tulips with Me" (inspired—falsetto and all—by the 1929 original version by Nick Lucas). This album went as high as #7 on the *Billboard* album chart, and led Tiny to his brilliant but short-lived television career. In addition to appearances on *Merv Griffin* and *Rowan & Martin's Laugh-In*, Tiny made true television history on *The Tonight Show* with Johnny Carson. Over the course of about two years, Tiny appeared as a *Tonight Show* guest more than a dozen times. His famous wedding ceremony to Miss Vicky on December 17, 1969, attracted a record 40 million viewers. In pictures of the ceremony, Tiny is holding Miss Vicky in one hand and his ukulele in the other.

While Tiny Tim's "fifteen minutes" ended pretty much after his wedding, he still continued to perform and record regularly until shortly before his death. In 1996, Tiny released a new CD on Rounder Records entitled *Girl*. He also guest-starred on the television show *Roseanne*. In concert, Tiny's uke playing was more of the three-chord variety, but his knowledge and passion for the great songwriters and singers of Tin Pan Alley was remarkable.

Ian Whitcomb
(JULY 10, 1941)

Tiny Tim is not the only guest of *The Tonight Show* to appear with a ukulele. In 1976, IAN WHITCOMB, originally from Surrey, England, also shared that distinction. While Whitcomb is still best known for his self-penned 1965 U.S. Top Ten hit "You Turn Me On," his real love has always been the roots of popular music, in particular, ragtime and the songs from

LET THE REST OF THE WORLD GO BY—
IAN WHITCOMB AND HIS BUNGALOW
BOYS (INTRODUCING: REGINA),
1991, ITW INDUSTRIES.
A PARTICULARLY GOOD EXAMPLE
OF THE WHITCOMB SOUND.
FEATURES PLENTY OF GREAT TIN PAN
ALLEY TUNES LIKE "MY CUTIE'S
DUE AT TWO-TO-TWO TODAY,"
AS WELL AS A WICKED TANGO VERSION
OF ROY ORBISON'S "OH! PRETTY
WOMAN," WITH UKE, OF COURSE!
COURTESY OF ITW INDUSTRIES

IAN ON *THE TONIGHT SHOW*
COURTESY OF
JOHNNY CARSON PRODUCTIONS.

the Tin Pan Alley era. Now living in Los Angeles, it's only fitting that Whitcomb maintains a busy schedule performing many of these songs on the ukulele.

Inspired by George Formby, Whitcomb picked up the uke at age fourteen. While he began playing the piano at an earlier age, the uke captivated him completely. When asked in 1996 what it was about the uke that he liked most, Whitcomb referred to its "jolly plangency" [resounding sound] and "bounce." As a performer, he feels playing the piano on stage is akin to being "stuck at a desk," while the far more portable uke allows him to "roam around." Whitcomb also admits that as a college student the uke was perfect for strumming in a car (as a passenger, we hope), and for serenading the fairer sex in the "secluded dunes" of some beach singing "You Were Meant For Me."

In addition to his many live performances, Whitcomb has published two uke songbooks, *Ukulele Heaven* and *Uke Ballads* and provided the soundtrack music for the films *Stanley's Gig* and Peter Bogdanovich's *Cat's Meow*.

IAN WHITCOMB

As a recording artist, he has released a number of highly-recommended CDs and cassettes that feature his uke strumming. As Whitcomb sings in "Do I Love You? — Yes, I Do!,"

from his 1991 release, *Let the Rest of the World Go By*, he replies, "I'll tell it to you daily, on my ukulele."

The Ukulele Orchestra of Great Britain

One of the brightest spots in the uke scene of the 1990s is the Ukulele Orchestra of Great Britain. Hugely successful in Japan, the Orchestra has gone, at times, without a record contract in its own country.

The Orchestra began life in 1985 with George Hinchliffe and Andy Astle, two art school chums. The pair had formed a performance art group called the Bronte Brothers that featured a lot of props and musical instruments. Dreaming of somehow being able to do an act that was

A FIST FULL OF UKULELES—THE UKULELE ORCHESTRA OF GREAT BRITAIN, 1993. RELEASED ON THEIR OWN LABEL, THIS RECORDING SHOWCASES THE ORCHESTRA IN ALL OF THEIR "DEPRAVED" GLORY. A GOOFY MIX OF CLASSICAL, NOVELTY AND CONTEMPORARY POP MUSIC. NOT TO BE MISSED ARE PRINCE'S "KISS," "JOHNNY B. GOODE," AND FELLOW UKE PLAYER JONI MITCHELL'S "A CASE OF YOU." COURTESY OF GEORGE HINCHLIFFE.

more "portable," they stumbled onto the idea of working ukuleles into the act. From that idea arose a group of twelve ukulele players, under the direction of Hinchliffe and Kitty Lux, who have taken the uke into the avant-garde. In the liner notes to their 1993 recording, *A Fist Full of Ukuleles*, they refer to their "depraved musicology" that has "alienated some traditionalists."

THE UKULELE ORCHESTRA OF GREAT BRITAIN.
COURTESY OF GEORGE HINCHLIFFE.

Since then, the Orchestra has taken its unique mix of deconstructed twenties songs, classical music, show tunes, and rock 'n' roll standards around the world. A typical set might include uke renditions of "Tonight" from *West Side Story*, Aretha Franklin's "Natural Woman," Tchaikovsky's "1812 Overture," the Troggs' "Wild Thing," and Chuck Berry's "Johnny B. Goode" with the lyric changed from "guitar" to "ukulele." Performances have included stops at the Chicago Music Festival, Hyde Park and Tokyo, Japan, where *A Fist Full Of Ukuleles* is a big hit.

UKE 'N' ROLL

Joni Mitchell began her musical career with a baritone uke. Tracy Chapman, Stephen Stills, David Byrne, Peter Frampton, Joan Baez and Chet Atkins have all admitted that the ukulele was an early musical influence.

JONI MITCHELL
PHOTOGRAPH COURTESY OF
LYNDON SMITH AND
THE MITCHELL FAMILY.

hootenanny.

"THERE IS A MEETIN' HERE TONIGHT......"

FEBRUARY 14 · 8:15pm

AT THE UNIVERSITY OF ALBERTA CALGARY

FEATURING: THE JUBILATION SINGERS from VANCOUVER, BILL ROBERTS from NORTH CAROLINA, WILL MILLAR from N.IRELAND, JONI ANDERSON from SASKATOON, PETER ELBLING from ENGLAND, SYDNEY McELVIE from DALLAS, TEXAS and THE TRANSIENTS from CALGARY.....

tickets: adults $1, students 50¢ at the bay box office, the depression and at the door.

THE ESSENTIAL UKULELE RECORD LIST

There have been a number of outstanding records that feature the ukulele. Unfortunately, many of them are out of print. Unless they are re-released, the best chance you have of finding most of the albums listed below is to call around to out-of-print record stores and go through boxes of used records at flea markets and garage/tag sales. Some of the artists listed are still putting out recordings (most in CD or cassette formats), and these are a little easier to find. Current records from Hawaii are usually available at record stores on the Islands. The list below represents records that the author has been able to find, and is by no means definitive.

It is, however, a good place to start.

Happy hunting and listening.

JOHN KAMEAALOHA ALMEIDA—
STRUM YOUR UKULELE, 49th State Hawaii Record Co.
c/o Cord International/Hana Ola Records.

EDDIE BUSH—A MAN AND HIS UKULELE,
Sea Shell Records.

CLIFF EDWARDS—UKULELE IKE SINGS AGAIN,
Disneyland Records.

CLIFF EDWARDS—SINGING IN THE RAIN,
1995, Audiophile Records.

GEORGE FORMBY—WITH MY UKULELE
(compilation), 1981, Decca.

ARTHUR GODFREY & HIS FRIENDS—
JAZZ FOR THE PEOPLE, Signature.

HOW ABOUT UKE? WIZARDS
OF THE UKULELE, Eddie Kamae, Ohta-San,
Jesse Kalima, Eddie Bush, Lehua Records.

KA'AU CRATER BOYS—ON FIRE!,
1994, Roy Sakuma Productions.

JESSE KALIMA—JESS UKE, SL5006,
Sounds of Hawaii (c/o Lehua Records).

JESSE KALIMA—LUAU TIME,
SL5004, Sounds of Hawaii (c/o Lehua Records).

EDDIE KAMAE—HEART OF THE UKULELE,
MS 3002, Mahalo Records (c/o Lehua Records).

EDDIE KAMAE AND THE SONS OF HAWAII—
THIS IS EDDIE KAMAE, Hula Records.

ISRAEL KAMAKAWIWO'OLE—FACING FUTURE,
1993, Bigboy Record Company.

MOE KEALE—IMAGINE, 1996, Pa'ani Records.

LEGENDS OF UKULELE—1998, Rhino Records

JOHNNY MARVIN: A VOICE OF THE '20S,
1987, Take Two Records.

KING BENNIE NAWAHI—
HOT HAWAIIAN GUITAR, 1928-1949, Yazoo Records.

OHTA-SAN— PACIFIC POT-POURRI ,
SL7005, Sounds of Hawaii (c/o Lehua Records).

OHTA-SAN—SONG FOR ANNA, A&M Records.

OHTA-SAN—UKULELE ISLE, Decca Records.

OHTA-SAN—WHERE IS MY LOVE TONIGHT,
1993, Roy Sakuma Productions, Inc.

LYLE RITZ—HOW ABOUT UKE?, Lyle Ritz
PLAYS JAZZ UKULELE, 1958, Verve Records.

LYLE RITZ—50TH STATE JAZZ, Lyle Ritz
AND HIS JAZZ UKULELE, 1959, Verve Records.

LYLE RITZ—TIME, 1995, Roy Sakuma Productions, Inc.

LYLE RITZ/HERB OHTA—A NIGHT OF UKULELE JAZZ/
LIVE AT MCCABE'S—2001, Flea Market Music

ROY SMECK—THE MAGIC UKULELE
OF ROY SMECK, ABC-Paramount.

ROY SMECK AND HIS MAGIC UKE, Kapp Records.

TINY TIM—GOD BLESS TINY TIM,
1968, Reprise Records.

JOHNNY UKULELE—FAVORITE SELECTIONS
BY JOHNNY UKULELE, Capitol Records.

THE UKULELE ORCHESTRA OF GREAT BRITAIN—
A FIST FULL OF UKULELES, 1993, Ukulele Orchestra of
Great Britain.

UKULELE STYLINGS 1 & 2, 1995, 1996, Pa'ani Records.

NELSON WAIKIKI—UKULELE STYLIST,
Tradewinds Records.

IAN WHITCOMB AND HIS BUNGALOW BOYS
(INTRODUCING: REGINA)—LET THE REST
OF THE WORLD GO BY, 1991, ITW Industries.

CHAPTER THREE

Made in Hawaii

Between 1885 and the 1915 Panama Pacific International Exposition, most of the machête and ukulele manufacturing was being done in Hawaii. By 1886, all three of the Portuguese woodworkers who came over on the *Ravenscrag* had opened instrument shops. These  *The Great Ukulele Manufacturers* men, Augusto Dias, Manuel Nunes and José do Espirito Santo, were handcrafting their instruments out of koa, some with a high degree of inlaid mother-of-pearl and other decorative touches. Prices for these were as little as $3, which at the time was the equivalent of a month's salary for a typical sugar plantation worker.

Then and now, the dominant wood used in the manufacture of Hawaiian ukes is koa wood, a large evergreen hardwood and member of the acacia family. According to M. Nunes & Sons' 1910 promotional materials, koa was found only in Hawaii and almost entirely on the island of Hawaii, the largest and most southerly of the island chain. Growing primarily at elevations of several thousand feet, koa was remarkable for its rich colorings of brown and gold and its beautiful grain. The choicest koa was "curly grained," and a great deal of effort went into hunting down trees with this characteristic. In the early years, it could take weeks to find these trees, cut them down, turn the wood into lumber and drag it out to a trail or road where it could then be carried by dray animals. Then, according to a 1916 Nunes ad, the koa wood was "naturally seasoned in Hawaii for years—not kiln dried."

According to his advertisements, Manuel Nunes was the "inventor" of the ukulele in 1879. By 1910, Manuel Nunes and his sons were making a full line of ukuleles, taropatches and steel guitars. The prices ranged from $10 for a plain koa wood uke to $35 for an "extra fancy curly koa wood" taropatch with inlay around the edges and sound hole. The six-string uke was another variation, with a doubling of two of the strings.

KOA TREES. HAWAII, CIRCA 1920.
COURTESY OF FREDERICK W. MCCONVILLE, BISHOP MUSEUM.

LEFT: LEONARDO NUNES' SIX-STRING; LEONARDO NUNES' STYLE 4 UKE; EARLY MANUEL NUNES' SOPRANO UKE; MANUEL NUNES' TAROPATCH.

LESLIE NUNES, GREAT GRANDSON
OF MANUEL NUNES, HOLDING
A 1910 MANUEL NUNES 8-STRING UKULELE
ON THE LEFT AND AN 1850 BRAGUINHA
MADE BY OCTAVIANNO NUNES
ON THE RIGHT.
PHOTOGRAPH BY ELIZABETH MAIHOCK BELOFF
—
ABOVE: MARTIN TAROPATCH
—
MANUEL NUNES TAROPATCH

THE TAROPATCH

The eight-string taropatch (or taro-patch fiddle) is a descendant of yet another Portuguese instrument known as the *rajao*, which was larger than the machête and had 5 individual strings. Legend has it that the *rajao* was embraced by the Hawaiian field workers who enjoyed playing the instrument on their work breaks. The *rajao* was renamed the taro-patch fiddle in honor of the "taro" plant that, when crushed, becomes poi, the Hawaiian food staple. Over time the *rajao* went from being a five-string instrument to a larger eight-string ukulele with four double courses of strings. It should be noted, however, that the taropatch is played and tuned like a soprano uke, just as a twelve-string guitar is played like the six-string version. In addition to Nunes, Martin made mahogany and koa taropatches between 1918 and 1931. Because of the increased difficulty in tuning as well as the pressing down of eight strings as opposed to four, the taropatch was far less popular than the standard uke.

In a 1946 "Paradise of the Pacific" article, Elma T. Cabral described how her grandfather, Augusto Dias, made ukuleles by hand: "Grandpa sawed koa into thin strips and wrapped it around a mold he had prepared. Gluing the edges, he tied cord around it to keep it in shape. Then he chiseled out an 'arm' that was to be glued to the main body. On this arm he made grooves, which were inlaid with strips of metal forming the musical scale. He drilled four holes on one end of the arm. Then he whittled four pegs to fit tightly into these holes. He cut thin strips of contrasting wood on the bias, gluing them around the edge of the instrument and around the large opening where the sound escaped. This was quite a feat and was done so skillfully that the joining of these strips could not be detected by the naked eye.

He sanded the instrument to satiny smoothness before he applied varnish. Catgut strings were knotted and attached to slots in the pegs and to those on a raised piece of wood on the opposite end of the instrument. After testing the scale and strumming a few chords to test its tone, Grandpa applied his seal on the inside of the instrument."

Today, ukuleles from the 1880s to 1910 are very scarce. This is due in part to the delicate nature of these instruments, but it also appears that comparatively few ukes were made in those early years. Santo continued to make instruments until he passed away in 1905. Dias retired in 1911 due to his tuberculosis. By 1910, however, the demand from Hawaii and the Mainland was strong enough that Nunes brought his sons into the business and they continued to make fine ukuleles until the mid 1930s.

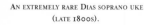

AN EXTREMELY RARE DIAS SOPRANO UKE
(LATE 1800S).

KUMALAE

KUMALAE'S 1915 PPIE
AND STYLE 3 UKES

In 1911, Jonah Kumalae started making ukes at the rate of 300 per month. Like most of the ukuleles made during this period, Kumalae ukes were considered finely made musical instruments. Kumalae took a booth at the 1915 Panama Pacific International Exposition to showcase his ukes and taropatches. As a result of his fine craftsmanship he received the P.P.I.E. Gold Award, which was a source of great pride. In addition to manufacturing ukuleles, Kumalae was also long active in local politics, poi making and newspaper publishing.

In the heyday of the 1930s, Kumalae's operation was a half-acre in size and employed 50 people. When Kumalae died in 1940, his uke business closed.

Today, the only early Hawaiian ukulele manufacturer still in business is Kamaka Hawaii, Inc. In 1910, Samuel K. Kamaka apprenticed himself to Manuel Nunes and learned the trade. Then in 1916 he established his own company in his basement workshop. By 1921, Kamaka had hired additional employees and

SAM JR. AND FRED KAMAKA
PHOTOGRAPH BY ELIZABETH MAIHOCK BELOFF

moved the business to a larger space. In 1959, Kamaka moved to its current address, a two-story factory at 550 South Street in Honolulu. Hand crafting as many as 4,000 instruments each year, Kamaka specializes in a variety of different koa ukuleles, including the standard

soprano, concert, tenor and baritone models. They also make six-string and eight-string Lili'u ukes as well as the famous "pineapple ukulele" that Sam designed in 1916. This particular uke has a bigger and warmer sound due to the larger body cavity, and some of the early painted versions are highly collectable.

One of the most interesting side notes to the Kamaka story is the fact that half of the twenty-two employees are hearing-impaired or deaf. Rather than being a handicap, it turns out that these uke builders are able to sense the perfect thickness of the koa by thumping the wood and feeling the vibration with their very experienced fingers.

According to legend, Sam Kamaka tried to make ukuleles out of twelve cigar boxes. Out of the twelve boxes, Kamaka was able to make seven good ukes. Two of them are pictured here.

Pineapple uke with painted front.

—

Left: Detail of Pineapple Style 3.

Mainland Manufacturers

They Came from Nazareth and Kalamazoo

Of all the Mainland ukulele manufacturers, the Martin name stands above all others. Established in 1833 by German émigré C. F. Martin, today the MARTIN GUITAR COMPANY of Nazareth, Pennsylvania, is world-renowned for their exceptional acoustic guitars. Nonetheless, the ukuleles that Martin made (and continues to make on special order) are without peer. Ironically, many of the great Hawaiian players have a special place in their hearts for ukes made by Martin.

Although the very first Martin ukuleles were put on the market in 1916, Frank Henry Martin (grandson of founder C. F. Martin) was already experimenting with uke-making as early as 1907. These experimental ukes were built more like small guitars with too much bracing and spruce tops. Not surprisingly, the tone was less than great and these ukes were not well received. The second time out, Martin used mahogany, which required less bracing, and the tone was much improved. Martin became so successful at making fine ukuleles that, during the peak years between 1916 and 1930, Martin doubled its work space and added employees to handle the uke demand.

Between 1916 and 1923, Martin made soprano mahogany ukes primarily. Then in 1923 they began making both mahogany and koa soprano-sized ukuleles in all styles. The easiest way to think of Martin uke styles is that the higher the number, the fancier the instrument. The Style 0, which was advertised as "plain, neat, serviceable," came only in mahogany and had the least amount of ornamentation. Styles 1 and 2, which also could be had in koa wood, were essentially the same as the Style 0 but with progressively more binding.

The Styles 3 and 5 were considered more for the professional player and are noted for their 17-fret, ebony fingerboard. The Style 3 featured even more decoration than the Style 2, and the Style 5K (the K is for koa) is considered by collectors to be one of the "holiest of grails," with elaborate pearl inlay in the fingerboard and in the head-stock. (The mahogany Style 5 was only made in 1941 and 1942.)

Martin also made a full line of different-sized ukes

Martin Model O

3K

5K

Oliver Ditson Dreadnought Style 3.

including the concert (beginning in 1925), tenor (1928) and baritone (1960). They also experimented with taropatches (made between 1918 and 1932) and ten-string uke-like instruments known as "tiples" (from 1919, with some versions still in the Martin line).

Martin also made a variety of ukuleles for other companies, including the Oliver Ditson Co., S.S. Stewart, Wurlitzer, Montgomery Ward, H.A. Weymann, Wm. J. Smith, Jenkins and Belltone companies.

STYLE 2
Stained mahogany body, top, and neck, ebony nut, rosewood fingerboard, patent pegs. Body bound front and back with ivory-celluloid.
Style 2-K. Similar in design, but body and top of Hawaiian koawood, natural color.

STYLE 3
Stained mahogany body, top, and neck, ivory nut and bridge-saddle, ebony finger-board, seventeen frets, pearl position marks, patent pegs, body ornamented with ivory-celluloid binding and inlay.
Style K-3. Similar in design, but body and top of Hawaiian koawood, natural color.
No. 3 and No. 3-K are designed for professional use.

STYLE 0
Natural finish mahogany body, top, and neck, hardwood finger-board and pegs, small position dots.
Plain, neat, serviceable.

STYLE 1
Stained mahogany body, top and neck, top bound with rosewood, narrow wood inlay, hardwood finger-board and pegs, small position dots.
Style 1-K. Similar in design, but body and top of Hawaiian koawood, natural color.

WILLIAM J. SMITH TIPLE.

THE 1940 MARTIN CATALOG IS AN EXAMPLE OF ELEGANT UNDERSTATEMENT. IN THE INTRODUCTION TO THE UKULELE SECTION, MARTIN INFORMS THE READER THAT THEIR UKES "ARE BUILT IN EIGHT STYLES, FOUR OF MAHOGANY AND FOUR OF HAWAIIAN KOA WOOD." ALL THE DESCRIPTIONS OF THE UKES ARE DEVOID OF THE MORE TYPICAL HARD-SELL LANGUAGE EXCEPT THE 5K. AT THE END OF THAT DESCRIPTION IT SAYS, "THE FINEST UKULELE MADE"—IN 1924 THE PRICE OF A 5K WAS $55. CATALOG COURTESY OF THE MARTIN COMPANY.

THE TIPLE

The ten-string tiple ("tiple" in Spanish means "little guitar") originated in Argentina. Lyon & Healy took credit for introducing this steel-string instrument to America in the mid-twenties. In their 1925 catalog, Lyon & Healy promoted the tiple (pronounced *tee-play* not *tip-ull*) in this way: "The tiple will appeal immediately to the advanced ukulele player. It enables him to play an entirely new instrument and with his knowledge of ukulele chords he can at once secure tonal effects of rare beauty and richness." There were two A strings (one regular, one an octave down), three D and F♯ strings (two regular with the middle one an octave lower), and two unison B's on the top. As a result, any uke player could play the tiple and get a very rich, full sound. The Martin tiple was designed in 1919 around an original brought back from Argentina by William J. Smith. This original used gut strings and was tuned like the top four strings of a guitar. Smith, who had his own music store in New York City, suggested to Martin that they make their own version. Martin reduced the body size, replaced the original gut strings with steel and tuned the instrument up to uke tuning.

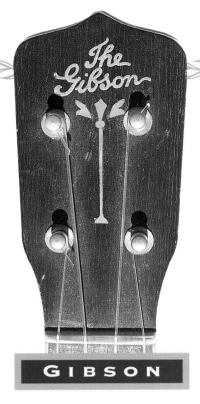

GIBSON

"...AFTER THE FIRST DESULTORY 'DRUMMING' ON ONE OF THE ORDINARY 'UKES' IS OVER, THERE COMES TO EVERY PLAYER A DESIRE TO OWN A BETTER INSTRUMENT... IT REMAINED FOR GIBSON TO DEVELOP A UKULELE OF THIS TYPE, EMBODYING THE FEATURES OF BEAUTY, RICH-NESS OF TONE, STURDY CONSTRUCTION AND TRUE SCALE." SO READ SOME OF THE "PURPLE" COPY IN GIBSON'S 1927 CATALOG OF "MANDOLINS, GUITARS & UKULELES." AS FOR THE STYLE UKE-3, THE CATALOG STATES, "NO FINER UKULELE HAS EVER BEEN OFFERED THAN THIS GIBSON WITH ITS DEEP, RICH MAHOGANY FINISH." WE ALSO LEARN ABOUT THE "SOUND-HOLE INLAID WITH PURFLING THAT HARMONIZES WITH THE FINISH; ROSEWOOD FINGER-BOARD BOUND IN WHITE AND INLAID WITH FANCY PEARL ORNAMENTS; SEVENTEEN NICKEL-SILVER FRETS; PEARL ORNAMENTS IN PEGHEAD, WITH 'THE GIBSON' IN BEAUTIFUL SILVER." IN 1927, THE STYLE 3 WAS PRICED AT $20. THE STYLE UKE-2 "EMBODIES THE SAME TONAL QUALITIES AS NO. 3," BUT "SOME OF THE DECORATIVE REFINEMENTS HAVE BEEN LEFT OFF TO DECREASE THE COST"—EXACTLY FIVE DOL-LARS WORTH. FOR TEN DOLLARS YOU COULD BUY STYLE UKE-1, WHICH WAS THE STRIPPED-DOWN MODEL.

GIBSON—STYLES 1, 3, 2.

Gibson is another famous Mainland musical instrument maker that made fine ukuleles. Begun in 1894 as Orville Gibson's one-man workshop, by 1902 the GIBSON MANDOLIN—GUITAR MANUFACTURING COMPANY, LIMITED of Kalamazoo, Michigan had 13 employees. While Gibson is best known for its acoustic and electric guitars, mandolins, and banjos, the company started making ukes in 1927 and also made a few ukulele banjos or banjo-ukes.

Gibson's Ukulele Styles 1, 2, and 3 differed in

ornamentation and fretboard length, with the Style 3 being the fanciest and having the longest fretboard. (Gibson also made ukuleles under the Recording King name.) In 1994, Gibson celebrated its 100th anniversary and continues to make fine musical instruments. Unfortunately, the Gibson ukulele line has been discontinued.

LEFT:
GIBSON BANJO UKE

RIGHT:
CIRCA 1931 GIBSON
"FLORENTINE" UKE.
COURTESY OF
STAN WERBIN
OF ELDERLY INSTRUMENTS.

The *Chicago Connection*

LYON & HEALY

Chicago was the home of a number of major musical instrument companies, many of whom made ukuleles. One of them was LYON & HEALY, who introduced the WASHBURN line in 1883. In addition to setting themselves up to mass produce their instruments (as opposed to Martin and Gibson, who emphasized hand crafting), Lyon & Healy also took credit for inventing the tenor guitar and bringing the tiple from South America to the U.S.

Lyon & Healy originally opened in 1864 as the Chicago branch of the Oliver Ditson Co., a major Boston-based musical instrument retailer. As retailers, Lyon & Healy offered the Kumalae and Nunes lines of ukuleles. In 1916, Lyon & Healy advertised Nunes ukuleles by saying they were "the favorite of college men and women everywhere…the most popular instrument of the day…and the fad of the hour."

As manufacturers, they offered a number of Washburn ukes and taropatches. In their 1923 catalog, five styles of ukes (three in koa) were offered. Later, they created their equivalent of the Martin 5K with the introduction of the famed koa Model 5320 Super Deluxe. This extra-fancy model featured binding front and back, a bound ebony fingerboard, and pearl inlay around the soundhole and in the fingerboard and headstock.

TOP: BELL TIPLE,
FAR LEFT: "CAMP" UKE,
RIGHT: "BELL" UKE,
DETAIL OF "CAMP" UKE.

One unusual Washburn uke offered from the mid-twenties to the mid-thirties was the Shrine Model (Models 5330 and 5331). For a much shorter time, the Bell Ukulele (No. 5325) was also produced. The Shrine was shaped like a balalaika and the Bell, of course, was bell-shaped. Also in the twenties and thirties, Washburn made both plain and fancy tenor ukes as well as tiples. For a short while, they even made the Bell Tiple (No. 5395).

In 1928 Lyon & Healy decided that its future was in retailing. As a result, all of the machinery and the rights to manufacture the Washburn line were sold to J. R. STEWART CO., another Chicago manufacturer. Three years earlier, the Stewart Co. had started making ukuleles and achieved success with its line of LeDomino ukes, featuring dominoes stenciled on the front of the instruments.

LYON & HEALY: "SHRINE" UKULELE, "DE LUXE MODEL," "VENETIAN UKE." ACCORDING TO THEIR 1925 CATALOG, THE "BELL" UKE WAS "A NEW DEPARTURE IN UKULELE DESIGN, ORIGINATED BY LYON & HEALY. THE UNIQUE SHAPE APPEALS IMMEDIATELY TO THE PURCHASER WHO IS SEEKING THE NOVEL AND INDIVIDUAL." THE SAME COULD ALSO BE SAID FOR A NUMBER OF ODDLY-SHAPED INSTRUMENTS THAT LYON & HEALY MANUFACTURED. FEATURED IN THE SAME CATALOG WERE THE TEARDROP-SHAPED "VENETIAN UKE," AND IN 1927 LYON & HEALY INTRODUCED THE "SHRINE" LINE OF GUITARS AND UKES. THE "CAMP UKE" LINE WAS DESIGNED FOR OUTDOOR USE AND, ACCORDING TO THE CATALOG, WAS PARTICULARLY GOOD FOR THE "NONE-TOO-CAREFUL TREATMENT YOUNG FOLKS ARE BOUND TO GIVE THEM." ILLUSTRATIONS SHOWED CAMP UKES BEING ENJOYED ON THE BEACH, IN A CANOE AND AROUND THE "CAMP" FIRE. THE "DE LUXE MODEL" WAS LYON & HEALY'S FANCIEST UKE, WHICH IN 1925 COST $25.

The Great Depression Hits

Unfortunately, the Stewart Co. had invested heavily in a new factory just prior to the stock market crash in October '29. When the Depression hit, they had no choice but to put the company up for sale. At auction, TONK BROS., a very successful Chicago-based wholesaler, bought the Washburn, Stewart and LeDomino trade names for a fraction of their pre-crash value. Tonk Bros. retained the Washburn brand and sold the Stewart and LeDomino names to another major Chicago manufacturer, the REGAL MUSICAL INSTRUMENT CO.

Established in 1914, the Regal Musical Instrument Co. made many inexpensive ukuleles throughout the twenties. Many of these were novelty instruments that featured cartoon characters and stenciled designs. In the thirties, Regal licensed the

REGAL

rights to manufacture and sell the Dobro brand, which included guitars, banjos and ukuleles.

An interesting sidebar to the Chicago guitar manufacturers' story is that, despite the competition, the various factories often built instruments for each other. For example, in the thirties, some of the later Washburn instruments were made by Regal. In 1954 Regal sold its manufacturing and trade names to yet another big Chicago manufacturer, Harmony.

FAR LEFT AND RIGHT: HAROLD TEEN—YELLOW AND HAROLD TEEN—GREEN UKES.

—

RIGHT: WENDELL HALL "TV" UKE.

ABOVE: CHARACTER DETAILS FROM HAROLD TEEN UKE SIT ATOP REGAL DOBRO.

"Touchdown," "Egyptian," "Cheer Leader" and "Whoopee."

—

Opposite page, clockwise from left:
"Art Moderne,"
"Art Moderne,"
"LeDomino" uke,
"Jungle Uke."

REGAL

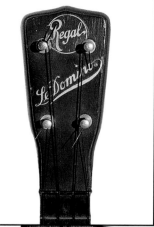

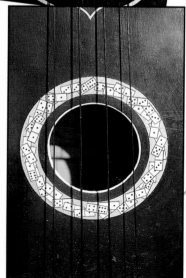

LEFT: DETAILS —
"LeDomino" UKE

REGAL

HARMONY

Begun in the late 1800s by Wilhelm J. F. Schultz, THE HARMONY CO. of Chicago had 125 employees by 1915 and was generating $250,000 in sales, mostly from guitars. After the 1915 Panama Pacific International Exposition, however, the ukulele exploded, and Harmony was the first large-scale manufacturer to jump into the uke business. In 1916 Sears & Roebuck bought Harmony, in an effort to acquire their uke production capability. By 1923, Harmony was producing a quarter of a million instruments per year, many of them ukes and banjo-ukes.

Another ukulele milestone occurred in 1928 when Harmony introduced its Roy Smeck Vita series of guitars and ukes, which featured pear-shaped bodies and seal-shaped soundholes. Johnny Marvin was another player who had his signature uke produced by Harmony. (See Chapter 2, *The Great Players and Personalities*). Other ukulele trade names made by Harmony included Stella, Supertone and Silvertone.

In 1941, Sears sold Harmony to a group of twelve employees who took the company to even greater heights. Much of their business came from manufacturing instruments with the trade names of dozens of other wholesalers, distributors and catalogue houses. At its peak in the mid sixties, Harmony had 600 employees and was making half of the country's guitars and three-quarters of all the ukuleles. Finally, due to increased competition from overseas, Harmony was liquidated in the mid seventies.

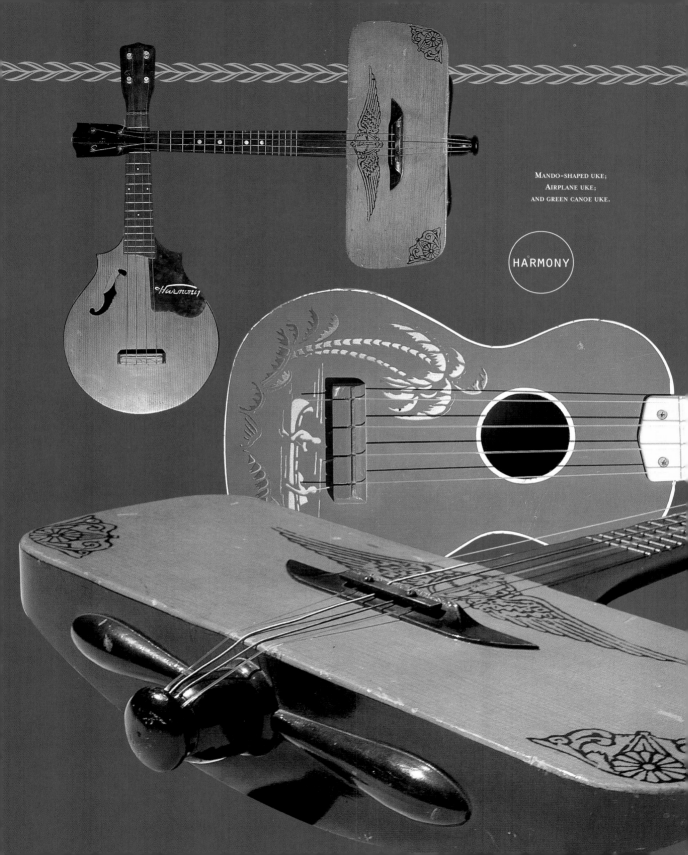

MANDO-SHAPED UKE;
AIRPLANE UKE;
AND GREEN CANOE UKE.

HARMONY

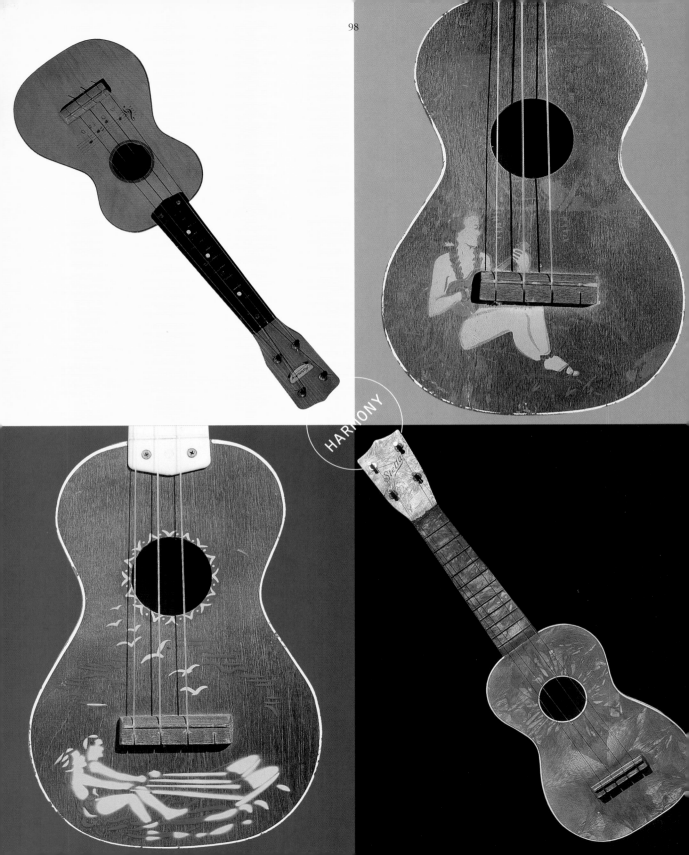

HARMONY

With some notable exceptions (i.e., the Vita and Johnny Marvin ukes), the Regal and Harmony ukes were more novelties than real musical instruments. That's not to say that they were unplayable or that they weren't a good first ukulele, but, at the time, they were created as an inexpensive and fun entry into the uke "craze." In 1932, one prominent catalog was selling many of these ukes for as little as $1.70. In the same catalog, the "Harold Teen" uke was $4.50 and the "Cheer Leader" was $4. In an ironic twist, many of today's uke collectors find these goofy ukes to be particularly attractive. To find an "Art Moderne" or "Jungle Uke" in good condition is sometimes more exciting than finding a much more "playable" Martin. The prices, too, for these unique instruments can be many, many times their original cost. Perhaps because they were so inexpensive, few buyers at the time worried very much about keeping them long term. This is why, despite the enormous number made, they are hard to come by nowadays.

QUITE A FEW OF THE UKES PICTURED HERE ARE EITHER THE SOLE UKE OFFERING OF A MANUFACTURER OR WERE MADE BY AN UNIDENTIFIABLE MEMBER OF THE "CHICAGO" FAMILY OF INSTRUMENT MAKERS. THERE IS SOMETHING ABOUT THE UKULELE THAT INSPIRED MANY INSTRUMENT MAKERS TO EXPERIMENT WITH THEIR DESIGNS.

—

LEFT TO RIGHT FROM TOP ROW: S. S. STEWART TAROPATCH, S. S. STEWART "MINI" UKE, HEART-SHAPED, NORTHERN, "SURF-A-LELE"; SWAGERTY LOGO, RICHTER, WABASH, BACON UKE; BRUNO, J. C. COWLE—5-STRING, GRETSCH—BLUE ROUND DETAIL, "IT" UKE; P'MICO "7-11" LUCKY UKE, GRETSCH—BLUE ROUND, DETAIL "NON-PAREIL" UKE, DEL VECCHIO MADE IN SÃO PAULO, BRAZIL.

CLOCKWISE FROM LEFT: COCOLELE, TURTURRO "TURNOVER" MANDO-UKE, KNUTSEN HARP-UKE, TURTURRO "PEANUT" UKE, "SURF-A-LELE" DETAIL.

The Ukelin

On occasion, this very
strange instrument shows
up at local flea markets.
Patented in 1926, the ukelin
was a cross between a violin
and a ukulele. It was played
on the lap by plucking the
zither-like strings with one
hand, while bowing a
completely different set of
strings with the other.
The sole manufacturer
of the ukelin was the
INTERNATIONAL MUSICAL
CORPORATION of
Hoboken, New Jersey.
They discontinued making
the ukelin in 1963.

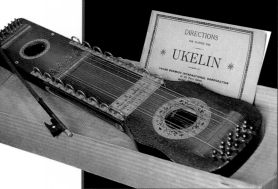

PHOTO COURTESY OF PAUL SYPHERS.

RIGHT: THREE FAVILLA TEARDROP UKULELES.
THE WIMBROLA—A SIX-STRING, 9-SIDED ODDITY—
WAS DESIGNED BY COLUMBIA BROADCASTING SYSTEM
RADIO STAR, DALE WIMBROW IN THE EARLY THIRTIES,
WEISSENBORN—UKULELE, HOLLYWOOD—PEARSON,
THREE CONCERT UKES AND A MINI-UKE.

ONE FROM

The FAVILLA GUITAR CO. began in Brooklyn, New
York, in 1890. Started by Italian émigrés John and
Joseph Favilla, Favilla Guitars also made its share of
ukes. In addition to making standard-sized ukes,

BROOKLYN, TWO FROM L.A.

Favilla also brought out their tear-shaped uke in a variety of colors. These ukes, like all Favilla instruments, always featured the family crest on the headstock. Herk (Hercules) Favilla, John Favilla's son, was a vaudeville performer who also worked at the factory. In 1951, Herk published a method book for the baritone uke (which Favilla was producing at the time) and in 1959 he took over the company. Due to rising costs, Favilla closed in 1973.

HERMANN C. WEISSENBORN emigrated from Germany to the United States in 1902, and settled in Los Angeles in 1910. Weissenborn did mostly violin and piano repair work through the 'teens; however, by the twenties he had jumped into the Hawaiian craze and was contributing his own lap steel guitars, guitars and ukes. The uke pictured below is a concert-sized uke. Like most Weissenborn instruments, it includes a branded shield on the wood, which can be seen through the soundhole, that says "H. Weissenborn, Los Angeles, Cal."

SCHIRESON BROS. instruments were designed and made in the late '20s and '30s by ROBERT E. PEARSON.

Some of his Hollywood ukuleles featured particularly fancy trim. Schireson also made a signature uke for Ray Canfield, a California-based performer, teacher and arranger. When Canfield arranged sheet music for uke, a logo of a ukulele appeared on the cover stating, "This copy contains a 'Ray Canfield' Symphonic Uke Arrangement."

FROM TOP:
DETAIL HOLLYWOOD UKE,
RAY CANFIELD LOGO-
(FROM "SAILIN' ON"), "RAY
CANFIELD" UKE.

THE METAL UKE

Some of the most remarkable ukuleles ever manufactured were made by the NATIONAL CO. Begun in 1925, the National String Instrument Corporation was formed by musician and inventor John Dopyera, a Czechoslovakian immigrant, with musician and vaudeville entertainer George Beauchamp (pronounced Bee-chum). Their idea was to make all-metal guitars, mandolins and ukuleles with resonators that would help make the instrument louder. At the time, ten years prior to the invention of the electric guitar, the acoustic guitar had a difficult time competing in volume with the other instruments in a typical vaudeville orchestra.

As a result of Beauchamp's interest in a louder guitar, Dopyera experimented with a variety of different aluminum alloys until he created the all-metal German-silver (or nickel silver—an alloy of copper, zinc and nickel) Hawaiian guitar. As for volume, Dopyera claimed it was seven times louder than a standard guitar. Due to a bitter dispute between Dopyera and Beauchamp over credit for the invention of the National guitar, Dopyera left the company in 1929 and proceeded to found the DOBRO COMPANY that same year—the five letters in the name Dobro refer to the five Dopyera Brothers, all of whom were involved in the business. The Dobro was another resonator-type instrument but designed around a convex rather a concave resonator.

Eventually, National ran into financial troubles

NATIONAL—STYLE 2.

and John Dopyera's brother Louis bought up the majority of the stock. On July 1, 1935, Dobro and National merged to form the NATIONAL DOBRO CORP., and in 1936 the newly combined company moved to Chicago. The strategy behind the move was to be near the big distributors and parts makers, as well as the new electronics firms who would provide parts for National Dobro's new venture into electric guitars. When the United States jumped into World War II, all peacetime industries converted to defense work, leading, ultimately, to the end of the National Dobro Corp.

Both National and Dobro made resonator ukuleles, and between 1928 and 1941, National made a large- and small-body uke in a variety of different styles. Styles 1, 2, and 3 featured German-silver bodies with (as the number got higher) ever more elaborate engravings on the front, back and sides. The Style 0 ukes featured Hawaiian designs sandblasted onto the metal body, while the less expensive Triolian line included a brown to yellow sunburst-paint- ed uke with a palm tree stenciled back. The Dobro uke came only in one style with a mahogany body. In 1933, Dobro licensed the Regal Company to make these instruments under the Dobro and Regal trade names.

In 1929, National was offering three different silver ukulele models; the Style 2, featuring engraving on the front, sides and back, sold for $70 at the time.

The Future's in Plastics

Between the years of 1949 and 1969, more than nine million plastic ukuleles were sold. The credit for this goes to a man named MARIO MACCAFERRI. Born in 1900 in northern Italy, Maccaferri began studying guitar at the age of nine. By the age of eleven he had apprenticed himself to Luigi Mozzani, a respected guitarist and luthier. At age twenty-one, Maccaferri had become known as a fine guitarist and was touring professionally throughout Italy.

During the Depression, Maccaferri, then living in Paris, turned to building guitars to supplement his income. It was during this time that he invented what became the Maccaferri-Selmer guitar, popularized by the famed Django Reinhardt. After breaking his hand in a swimming pool accident, Maccaferri had to give up performing and thus turned his attention to inventing. The "Maccaferri Isovibrant" clarinet reed was one of his earlier innovations.

In the late forties, having moved his reed operation to New York City, Maccaferri became

intrigued with the potential of plastic. At first, when cane became hard to find during World War II, he found success manufacturing plastic clarinet reeds. Acceptance came quickly thanks to an endorsement from famed clarinetist Benny Goodman. Eager to further his forays into plastic, Maccaferri combined his knowledge of plastics lineage and guitar building and in 1949 introduced the Islander ukulele. Patterned after a Martin Style 0, Maccaferri priced his all-plastic uke at $5.95 (in 1952, due to increased production efficiencies, Maccaferri was able to lower the price 33% to $3.95). Despite its plastic lineage, the Islander was a remarkably good instrument: it was easy to play, easy to tune, and even more remarkably, it had a warm tone.

Once again, good fortune shone on Maccaferri, thanks to a high profile endorser. Early on, Arthur Godfrey got a hold of an Islander and plugged it on his TV show (see Chapter Two, *The Great Players and Personalities*). The next day, Maccaferri was deluged with phone calls. Because of Godfrey's unsolicited enthusiasm, Maccaferri suddenly had more than 150,000 back orders. He managed to fill these, and went on to sell millions of plastic ukes.

Over the years, Maccaferri's company, MASTRO INDUSTRIES, created a variety of different ukes and uke accessories. In 1951, the uke line included the Islander at $5.95, the slightly larger and fancier Islander Deluxe priced at $7.95

and the kid-sized Sparkle Plenty Islander Ukette priced at $2.98 (Sparkle Plenty was the child in the very popular Dick Tracy comic strip). Included with the two larger ukes were a book called *Godfrey The Great: The Life Story of Arthur Godfrey*, a method and songbook by May Singhi Breen and a felt pick. A nifty accessory was something called the Islander Visual Chordmaster, which, when attached to the fretboard, allowed the player to make many of the most basic chords with the push of a button.

In 1953, Maccaferri introduced the Islander Baritone Ukulele priced at $12.95. He also brought out the T.V. Pal at $1.75, which was a lower-cost version of the soprano-sized Islander. In 1965 the Mastro catalog included a full line of ukes, a banjo uke and a banjolele. In 1969, at the age of 69, Maccaferri finally got out of the plastic musical instrument business and sold off most of his molds to Carnival, another plastic novelty maker.

PLASTIC UKES— FLAMINGO BROWN, ISLANDER UKE, FIN-DER UKE, CARNIVAL, ISLANDER. THE "FIN-DER" WAS A PLASTIC UKE CREATED BY GEORGE A. FINDER AND DEVELOPED BY NINO MARCELLI IN 1950. BASED IN SAN DIEGO, FIN-DER INC. OFFERED THIS WEST COAST-INFLUENCED UKE WITH "FIN-DER BEACH BOY GENUINE NYLON, COLORED UKULELE STRINGS." THE FOUR STRING COLORS WERE RED HIBISCUS, BLUE IRIS, GREEN FERN AND ORANGE GINGER.

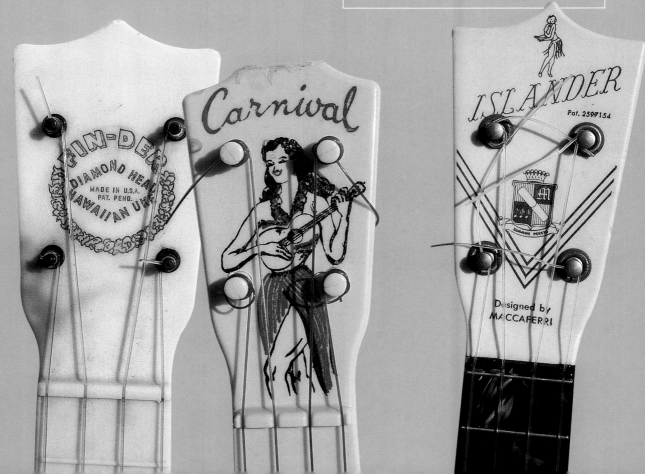

CHAPTER FOUR

Uke Can Change the World

Due to its ease of play, portability and association with a paradise-like place, the ukulele has traveled all over the globe. While uke players can be found in many corners of the world, Japan and Canada have especially interesting associations with the instrument. This is mostly due to one person in each country who had a grand vision of what might be accomplished with just a small musical instrument with four strings.

The Story Continues ...

OPPOSITE: ILLUSTRATION BY ROBERT ARMSTRONG 2002
ABOVE: STARS FLUKE

JAPAN

On June 6, 1999 the Nihon Ukulele Association (NUA) based in Tokyo, Japan celebrated its 40th anniversary. The first half of the event was comprised of formal presentations on the history of NUA, as well as lectures on the history of the ukulele and its best known players and personalities. During this portion, held in a beautiful, top-floor conference room at the famed Yamano Music Co. in the Ginza district, it was clear that NUA was very proud of its long association with the ukulele. Afterwards, at a party in a Tokyo beer garden, the seriousness of the event gave way to joy as hundreds of members and their guests collectively and individually strummed their ukuleles into the night.

NUA was the creation of Yukihiko "Harry" Haida (1909-1985) who saw the ukulele as an easy-to-play musical instrument for amateurs. Haida, who was born in Hawaii as a second-generation Japanese (Nisei), moved to Japan at the age of twelve when his father died. Having brought a love of Hawaiian music with him to Japan, Haida and his brother Katsuhiko in 1929 formed the Moana Glee Club, a group dedicated to performing Hawaiian music. Part of the rapid acceptance of the group was due to the overall enthusiasm for Western popular music at the time, especially Hawaiian music and jazz.

While most Western music was banned by the authorities during World War II, fans and players continued to keep it alive in secret. After the war,

BORN IN JAPAN IN 1955, KAZUYUKI SEKIGUCHI IS THE BASSIST OF THE POPULAR JAPANESE ROCK GROUP, THE SOUTHERN ALL STARS. IN 1993, HE PUBLISHED A BOOK ON THE UKE ENTITLED *THE EPICUREAN UKULELE* AND IN 1997 HE PRODUCED *UKULELE CALENDAR*, THE FIRST UKULELE COMPILATION CD IN JAPAN. THAT SAME YEAR HE PUBLISHED HIS SECOND UKE BOOK, *UKULELE LOVE*. HE HAS ALSO PRODUCED TWO HERB OHTA INSTRUCTIONAL VIDEOS.

the love affair resumed to an even greater degree. In 1953, Harry Haida discovered Herb Ohta, a young Hawaiian Marine Corps interpreter based in Japan, who played the ukulele as a solo instrument. This meeting led to Ohta's first record for the Nihon Victor Company (JVC) where Haida had also made his own solo ukulele recordings. It was this association with Ohta that inspired Haida to create NUA in 1959.

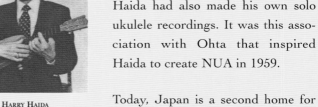

HARRY HAIDA

Today, Japan is a second home for Hawaiian musicians and ukulele virtuosos. Herb Ohta and next-generation players like Herb Ohta, Jr. and Jake Shimabukuro regularly tour there. Also, home grown players IWAO, Kazuyuki Sekiguchi and uke groups like Petty Booka have released popular ukulele recordings.

ROLLING COCONUTS MAGAZINE #4 CIRCA 1999

THE COVER ALWAYS INCLUDES "THIS IS FREE MAGAZINE OF UKULELE WORLD." THIS SMALL MAGAZINE COVERS THE JAPANESE UKULELE SCENE, AND INCLUDES FEATURES ON PLAYERS, TIPS ON PLAYING, REVIEWS AND ADVERTISEMENTS. (COURTESY OF ROLLING COCONUTS).

CANADA

As Director of Music Education in Halifax, Nova Scotia, throughout the 1970s, J. Chalmers Doane was responsible for thousands of children and

adults learning to play the ukulele. Taught by his mother, Doane began playing uke at the age of four and went on to develop skills on a variety of musical instruments. He graduated as a trombone major and string education specialist from Boston University. It was his profound belief in the value of

J. CHALMERS DOANE
HOLDING ONE OF HIS UNIQUE
TRIANGULAR UKULELES.

the ukulele, however, for which he is best known.

Beginning with a program in the Halifax elementary public schools, he ultimately crafted a method that not only inspired students to learn music through the ukulele but, even more importantly, taught teachers to effectively pass it on. At the program's peak there were 50,000 schoolchildren and adults learning uke throughout Canada and in some parts of the United States, including Florida and Hawaii. At the same time his top players in the "A" group were performing in

concert and making self-subsidized recordings. Doane published the magazine *Ukulele Yes!* aimed at both teachers and students and helped design the distinctive, triangular-shaped Northern ukulele.

For Doane the ukulele was a means to two ends: One was his belief that learning the ukulele was an unusually good way to teach young people to become musicians. Thus his emphasis on music theory, sight-reading, eartraining, singing, solo and ensemble playing. At the same time, Doane saw the ukulele as a serious musical instrument capable of providing a great deal of personal joy. Though retired, Doane is still teaching ukulele, performing and recording.

CLASSROOM UKULELE METHOD
BY J. CHALMERS DOANE
1980 REVISED EDITION
WATERLOO MUSIC CO., LTD.

ORIGINALLY PUBLISHED IN 1971, THIS WAS
CONSIDERED CANADA'S FOREMOST TEXT FOR
CLASSROOM UKULELE INSTRUCTION. DOANE
WRITES, "THIS BOOK WAS WRITTEN SO THAT YOU
AND YOUR STUDENTS MAY HAVE MORE FUN WITH
MUSIC. PLEASE DO JUST THAT!"

HALIFAX UKULELES & FIDDLES
RECORD ALBUM
1979 WATERLOO MUSIC CO., LTD.

AN EXCITING DEMONSTRATION OF THE TOP UKULELE AND
VIOLIN STUDENT PLAYERS FROM THE HALIFAX SCHOOL
SYSTEM UNDER THE DIRECTION OF J. CHALMERS DOANE.
IT FEATURES UKE ENSEMBLE ARRANGEMENTS OF POP
STANDARDS LIKE "LULLABY OF BIRDLAND,"
"THE SHADOW OF YOUR SMILE," "CLOSE TO YOU"
AND DOANE ORIGINAL, "NEW YORK STRUM."

BACKGROUND IMAGE:
UNKNOWN CANDID
(COURTESY OF CHUCK FAYNE)

Other Historical Images

Since the first edition, many more great uke-related and historical images have been unearthed. For your viewing pleasure...

PROMOTIONAL PHOTO OF MARIO MACCAFERRI
AND THE WATERPROOF ISLANDER PLASTIC UKULELE IN A FISH TANK.
(PHOTO COURTESY OF MARIA MACCAFERRI)

1951 JANTZEN MAGAZINE AD
(COURTESY OF JANTZEN, INC.)

for glamour...

and l'amour...

...there's nothing like a Jantzen!

the next best thing to going to Tahiti this summer
is to go Tahitian...and what it takes to go Tahitian
only Jantzen can give you...romantic, exotic
cabana jobs like this...the happiest happy talk
prints painted in Tahiti...so perfect in mood...

PANAMA-PACIFIC INTERNATIONAL EXPOSITION, SAN FRANCISCO, 1915.

IT'S AN INTERESTING COINCIDENCE THAT THE UKULELE FIGURES INTO THREE
HISTORIC EXPEDITIONS. UKULELES TRAVELED ON BOTH THE ARCTIC AND
ANTARCTIC EXPEDITIONS OF COMMANDER ROBERT E. BYRD. DICK KONTER
(SEE PAGE 57) SMUGGLED A MARTIN 0 UKULELE ABOARD THE PLANE THAT FLEW
OVER THE NORTH POLE IN 1926. KONTER ALSO BROUGHT A UKE AND HAD A
DOZEN OR SO FAVILLA UKULELES SENT TO HIM DURING THE 1929–1930
ANTARCTICA EXPEDITION. SIMILAR TO THE MARTIN 0, ONE OF THESE UKES WAS
SIGNED BY MEMBERS OF THE TEAM AND INCLUDES BYRD'S SIGNATURE ON THE
HEADSTOCK. EVENTUALLY, THE UKULELE WAS GIVEN TO FAVILLA BROS.
IN GRATITUDE.

THE PHOTO OF NEIL ARMSTRONG (ABOVE) WAS TAKEN BY DON BLAIR ON JULY
24TH, 1969 AT ABOUT 10PM ON THE USS HORNET. IT WAS TAKEN THE FIRST
NIGHT THAT ARMSTRONG, EDWIN "BUZZ" ALDRIN AND MIKE COLLINS SPENT IN
THE MQF (MANNED QUARANTINE FACILITY) AFTER HAVING RETURNED FROM THE
MOON MISSION. THEY WOULD STAY THERE FOR THREE WEEKS WHILE BEING
CHECKED FOR POSSIBLE "MOON GERMS." BLAIR, A RADIO POOL CORRESPONDENT,
HAPPENED TO BE WALKING BY AT JUST THE RIGHT MOMENT AND TOOK THIS
PICTURE OF ARMSTRONG WITH HIS UKE.
(PHOTO OF FAVILLA UKE COURTESY OF TOM FAVILLA)
(PHOTO OF NEIL ARMSTRONG COURTESY OF DON BLAIR)

1903. THE HAWAIIAN PAVILION.

HAWAIIAN PAVILION
POSTCARD OF THE HAWAIIAN PAVILION AT THE 1915 PANAMA-PACIFIC INTERNATIONAL EXPOSIT
THIS WAS WHERE MILLIONS OF MAINLANDERS HAD THEIR FIRST TASTE OF HAWAIIAN SONGS
DANCE AND UKULELES.

Pop Culture Visibility

At the turn of the millennium, the ukulele appeared in all sorts of places. Thanks to the endless fascination with the first cast of the CBS television reality show, *Survivor*, the ukulele received an unexpected amount of press as the "personal item" that contestant Sonja Christopher took with her to Pulau Tiga off the coast of Borneo. In what she referred to as a "blessing in disguise," Christopher and her baritone uke were the first to be voted off the island.

SONJA CHRISTOPHER. FIRST PERSON VOTED OFF THE ISLAND IN THE VERY FIRST EPISODE OF *SURVIVOR*. (COURTESY OF SONJA CHRISTOPHER)

The ukulele was also prominently featured in Disney's *Lilo & Stitch*, their 2002 animated film set in Hawaii. Included in the avalanche of movie tie-in merchandise were images of Lilo strumming her uke in a hammock and even an official plastic *Lilo & Stitch* uke.

The ukulele is also the instrument of choice for the star of the hip and popular Nickelodeon cartoon *SpongeBob SquarePants*. SpongeBob has all sorts of adventures in his sea-bottom town, and the soundtrack has a humorous, retro-Hawaiian quality.

...And More

The ukulele continues to be at the center of more and more festivals. In addition to the annual Ukulele Festival in Honolulu, The Ukulele Hall of Fame Museum's Ukulele Expo, and the Hayward (California) Uke Festival, there are various other one-day events taking place in Cerritos, California, San Antonio, Texas, and Seattle, Washington.

Concerts featuring a variety of uke-playing performers attract a devoted audience of fans and other players. "UKEtopia," which describes itself as a "Ukulele Heaven on Earth," is held annually at the legendary McCabe's Guitar Shop in Santa Monica, California. Debuting in 1998, and produced by Jim and Liz Beloff, this show has featured uke entertainers from Los Angeles and beyond, including the Beloffs, Ian Whitcomb, Travis Harrelson, Chuck Fayne, Bill Tapia, Larry D., Shep Stern, King Kukulele, Janet Klein, Rick Cunha, Lyle Ritz, Peter Brooke Turner, Ukulele Dick, John Zehnder and others. A concert entitled "New Uke, New York" was held at Joe's Pub in New York City in 2001. That show presented New York-based performers, Songs from a Random House, White Knuckle Sandwich, The Moonlighters, Miss Ewa's Hawaiian Trio and The Haoles.

Rock That Uke, a documentary focusing on post-punk uke players, was screened at the 2002 Ukulele Expo. Directed by William Preston Robertson and Sean Anderson, the film featured interviews and performances with alternative players all across the continental United States. According to the directors, RTU asks, "Is there a ukulele personality? And if so, what compels a person to electronically distort this little instrument and play loud, aggressive music?"

The Stamford (Connecticut) Museum and Nature Center mounted a major exhibit to examine the history of the ukulele. *Ukulele Fever* opened in February 2002 and featured over 100 vintage and contemporary ukuleles. Also, *The Ukulele Occasional*, a magazine dedicated to ukulele history and culture, debuted in the summer of 2002.

TOP: UKE STICKER (COURTESY OF TIKI KING); UKE 2002 POSTCARD (COURTESY OF UKULELE HALL OF FAME MUSEUM)
MIDDLE: UKULELE FESTIVAL STICKER (COURTESY OF ROY SAKUMA PRODUCTIONS)
BOTTOM: NEW UKE, NEW YORK POSTCARD (ILLUSTRATION BY JENNIFER PEREZ);
THE UKULELE OCCASIONAL

Current Ukulele Songbooks

The renewed interest in the ukulele has also inspired a steady stream of new songbooks.

JUMPIN' JIM'S SONGBOOKS/VIDEO:

THERE ARE MORE THAN A DOZEN JUMPIN' JIM'S SONGBOOKS IN PRINT COVERING VARIOUS MUSICAL GENRES, INCLUDING TIN PAN ALLEY, HAWAIIAN HAPA-HAOLE SONGS, SIXTIES TUNES, CAMP SONGS, BEACH SONGS, GOSPEL SONGS AND MOVIE THEMES. SONGBOOKS ARRANGED BY LEGENDARY PLAYERS HERB OHTA AND LYLE RITZ INCLUDE CDS OF THE ARRANGERS PERFORMING THE TUNES.
(COURTESY OF FLEA MARKET MUSIC, INC.)

JUMPIN' JIM'S TIPS 'N' TUNES (1994)
JUMPIN' JIM'S GONE HAWAIIAN (1999)
JUMPIN' JIM'S '60S UKE-IN (1999)
JUMPIN' JIM'S UKULELE MASTERS: LYLE RITZ JAZZ (2000)
JUMPIN' JIM'S UKULELE MASTERS: HERB OHTA (2002)

THE JOY OF UKE — TAUGHT BY JUMPIN' JIM BELOFF
HOMESPUN VIDEO, 1998. A HOW-TO-PLAY VIDEO. INCLUDES SPECIAL GUESTS PONCIE PONCE, TRAVIS HARRELSON AND IAN WHITCOMB.
(COURTESY OF HOMESPUN VIDEO)

OTHER MAINLAND AND HAWAIIAN BOOKS:

UKULELE HEAVEN
MEL BAY PUBLICATIONS, 1999. COMPILED, WRITTEN & PRODUCED BY IAN WHITCOMB
A BOOK/CD FILLED WITH "SONGS FROM THE GOLDEN AGE OF THE UKULELE," PLUS EIGHT NEW WHITCOMB TUNES.
(COURTESY OF MEL BAY PUBLICATIONS)

TREASURY OF UKULELE CHORDS
ROY SAKUMA PRODUCTIONS, 1998. BY ROY SAKUMA
OVER 800 CHORD DIAGRAMS!
(COURTESY OF ROY SAKUMA PRODUCTIONS)

HOW TO PLAY THE HAWAIIAN UKULELE—10 EASY LESSONS
MUTUAL PUBLISHING, 2000.
THOROUGH METHOD BOOK PUT OUT BY THE UNIVERSITY OF HAWAII
(COURTESY OF MUTUAL PUBLISHING)

HAWAIIAN UKULELE: THE EARLY METHODS
CENTERBROOK PUBLISHING, 1998.
BOOK CONTAINS REPRINTS OF NINE EARLY HOW-TO-PLAY BOOKS.
(COURTESY OF CENTERBROOK PUBLISHING)

INTERNATIONAL UKULELE BOOKS AND PERIODICALS:

GERMANY

TOTAL UKULELE
VOGGENREITER VERLAG 2001, (ENGLISH EDITION) 2002
GERNOT RODDER
UKULELE METHOD BOOK WITH CD. FEATURES A WIDE RANGE OF MATERIAL INCLUDING A GERMAN FOLKSONG, A BLUES TUNE AND A UKE DUET OF BACH'S "BOURRÉE" FROM THE LUTE SUITE IN E MINOR.

FRANCE

LA MÉTHODE D'UKULELE BY CYRIL LEFEBVRE
BAND A PART 2001
DELIGHTFUL, WELL-DESIGNED OVERVIEW WITH A LOT OF GREAT PHOTOS, UKE HISTORY, EXERCISES AND SONGS INCLUDING LEFEBVRE ORIGINALS, WITH CD.

SWEDEN

STORA UKULELE SKOLAN
1997 SWEDISH UKULELE METHOD BOOK WRITTEN BY THOMAS ALLANDER

HOLLAND

LIEDJES VOOR UKULELE
1961 DUTCH UKULELE SONGBOOK

JAPAN

BOO TAKAGI UKULELE METHOD BOOK
BOO TAKAGI IS A WELL-KNOWN JAPANESE COMEDIAN AND UKULELE PLAYER. WHEN HE GAVE UKULELE LESSONS ON THE JAPANESE NHK TELEVISION NETWORK IN 1999, HE SPURRED A LOT OF UKULELE SALES.

Ukulele in the Title

Favorite collectibles for uke fans
are songs and sheet music that have
"ukulele" in the title.

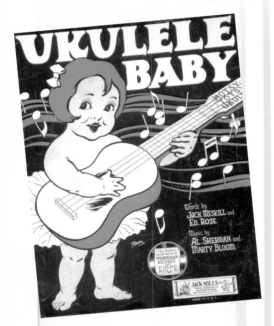

Ukulele Art

The ukulele has also proved to be a suitable canvas and subject for visual artists. For some, it can be deconstructed and turned into a work of art. For others, it provides a great surface on which to place bold and fun images.

FAR LEFT COLUMN:

"UKULELE BABY," 1925
WORDS BY JACK MESKILL AND ED ROSE
MUSIC BY AL SHERMAN AND MARTY BLOOM
JACK MILLS MUSIC PUBLISHERS
THE UKULELE HAS GOTTEN IN BETWEEN THE
SINGER OF THIS SONG AND THE OBJECT OF HIS
DESIRE, WHO WON'T STOP STRUMMING.

"HE PLAYED HIS UKULELE AS THE SHIP WENT
DOWN," 1932
BY ARTHUR LE CLERQ
CAMPBELL, CONNELLY & CO., LTD., LONDON
COMEDY SONG WITH MULTIPLE CHORUSES.

MIDDLE COLUMN:

"UKULELE DREAM-MAN," 1926
BY LEE STERLING & REED STAMPA
WORTON DAVID, LTD., LONDON

"YOU CAN'T PLAY MY UKULELE," 1933
BY AL HOFFMAN, AL GOODHART AND RALPH BLUE
KORNHEISER AND SCHUSTER
"YOU CAN'T PLAY MY UKULELE TO SING YOUR SONGS
TO SOMEBODY ELSE, WHEN I SING MINE TO NOBODY
ELSE BUT YOU."

"ON MY UKULELE (TRA LA LA LA LA)," 1924
WORDS AND MUSIC BY MITCHELL PARISH,
MIKE MORRIS AND LOU HERSCHER
JOE MORRIS MUSIC CO.
COMEDY SONG WITH 18 VERSES AND A
"UKULELE/GAILY" RHYME.

"SO I PICKS UP MY UKULELE (AND I SINGS HER A
LITTLE SONG)," 1930
BY MITCHELL PARISH, STEVE NELSON, JOHNNY BURKE
MILLS MUSIC, INC.
COMEDY SONG WITH THE TITLE BEING A SOLUTION
FOR ALL KINDS OF ROMANTIC SITUATIONS.

RIGHT COLUMN:

"UKULELE DREAM GIRL," 1926
WORDS AND MUSIC BY REG LOW
FRANCIS, DAY & HUNTER, LTD., LONDON

"UKULELE MOON," 1930
LYRIC BY BENNY DAVIS, MUSIC BY CON CONRAD
LEO FEIST, INC.
NOTABLE RHYME: PALMS/ARMS

"THE GHOST OF THE UKULELE," 1916
BY JAMES BROCKMAN AND JACK SMITH
"...HOW THEY SWAY WHEN THEY PLAY ON THE GAY
LITTLE UKULELE PLAYING DAILY."

"UKALELE DALY," 1915
WORDS BY WM. JEROME AND HARRY WILLIAMS
MUSIC BY JEAN SCHWARTZ
UKALELE DALY HAS STRAYED FROM THE EMERALD
ISLE TO THE HAWAIIAN ISLE. HE'S LEFT MOLLY
RYAN IN KILLARNEY, WHO ADVISES HIM TO "THROW
AWAY YOUR UKALELE...AND COME BACK TO ME."

FROM LEFT TO RIGHT:
SUBMARINE UKE BY HARRY F. EIBERT
TIKI FLUKE BY TIKI KING (PHOTO BY SANDOR NAGYSZALANCZY)
PAINTED PICASSO SOPRANO UKE BY DUANE HEILMAN
POOCH-A-LELE HANDPAINTED BY ROBERT ARMSTRONG 2002
THE CABINET OF CURIOSITIES – UKULELE SERIES BOOK #15 BY PETER & DONNA THOMAS 2002
BANANA SOPRANO UKE BY DUANE HEILMAN
SPAM-A-LELE – THE UKULELE AS AN ICON SERIES BY KEITH S. BRAMER

More Notable Strummers

The biggest news continues to be about former Beatle George Harrison's enthusiasm for the uke. His posthumous CD *Brainwashed* included plenty of strumming, especially on the remake of the classic song "The Devil and the Deep Blue Sea." In the many articles that came out after his death, some of his closest friends referred to his love of the uke. In an interview in the January 17, 2002 issue of *Rolling Stone*, fellow Traveling Wilbury, Tom Petty, talked a good bit about Harrison's obsession with the uke. In fact, Petty did some strumming of his own on the song "The Man Who Loves Women" from his 2002 CD release, *The Last DJ*.

Paul McCartney, in his hugely successful 2002 U.S. tour, included a performance of Harrison's "Something" on a Gibson ukulele that George had given him. For many who attended those concerts, it was a great example of the kind of sweet music one man and a ukulele can make. It also inspired many to look into playing a uke themselves.

Pearl Jam lead singer and guitarist Eddie Vedder has also been writing and performing with a ukulele. In an interview in the debut issue of *The Ukulele Occasional*, he admitted to "finding little melodies" in the uke that led to the writing of "Soon Forget," a song recorded with just voice and uke on Pearl Jam's *Binaural* CD.

Bill Tapia

Bill "Tappy" Tapia was born in Honolulu on January 1, 1908 (incredibly, Tapia's mother, father and aunt were all born on January first). At the age of seven, he learned a few chords from a neighbor and quickly became a good player. The next

ABOVE: BILL TAPIA 2001 (PHOTO BY ELIZABETH MAIHOCK BELOFF); BACKGROUND IMAGE: BILL TAPIA WITH WHITE KAMAKA PINEAPPLE UKE 1938 (PHOTO BY FRANK M. LAI)

year he bought his first uke, a Nunes, for 75 cents. A very resourceful young man, Tapia was soon earning money strumming at USO shows for WWI troops, at local vaudeville and silent movie theaters and, later, on cruise ships. By the age of thirteen, he had already played with Hawaiian musical legends Sol Hoopi'i, King Bennie Nawahi and Ernest Kaai.

Although he became better known for his jazz guitar playing, Tapia strummed his way into a bit of ukulele history. Most notable was his playing at the opening night party of the famed Royal Hawaiian Hotel in Waikiki. The year was 1927 and Tapia was the banjo and uke player in Johnny Noble's band, hired for the occasion. During the 'twenties and 'thirties, while living and working in both Hawaii and California, Tapia gave ukulele lessons to celebrities such as Shirley Temple, Clark Gable and Jimmy Durante. He also wrote and arranged the method book *Hawaiian Ukulele Instructions* for the ukulele manufacturer Ka-lae. On January 1, 2003, Bill turned 95 and spent the day at his home strumming his uke for gathered family, friends and current uke students.

1936 KA-LAE METHOD BOOK ARRANGED BY BILL TAPIA

Travis Harrelson

Travis Harrelson is a fixture of the Southern California uke world. Known for a unique and complex strum, his right-hand work is difficult to describe, let alone imitate. Harrelson grew up in Long Beach, California, and learned the ukulele as a result of his mother, who loved all things Hawaiian. Over many years he developed his style of playing as well as a deep love of classic Tin Pan Alley and hapa-haole songs. He also built up an

TRAVIS HARRELSON ABOARD THE U.S. PRINCETON AIRCRAFT CARRIER IN 195

enviable collection of rare vintage ukes. He performs regularly at Hawaiian music and dance festivals in Southern California and along with this author conducts workshops at McCabe's Guitar Shop in Santa Monica. An example of his unique strumming can be seen in *The Joy of Uke* video with Jim Beloff.

Byron Yasui, Gordon Marks and Benny Chong

Featured on *The Art of Solo 'Ukulele* along with Jake Shimabukuro, these three Hawaiian virtuosi each have a long list of musical credits. Benny Chong is known as the guitarist for the Don Ho show. He has played ukulele since childhood and

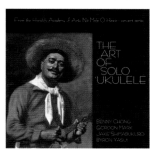

was most influenced by Lyle Ritz's breakthrough jazz uke recordings on Verve. On this CD, he performs remarkably rich and full solo arrangements of pop standards like "The Way You Look Tonight" and "All The Things You Are." Gordon Marks makes his recording debut here with solo ukulele arrangements of classical works like the "Love Theme" from Tchaikovsky's *Romeo and Juliet* and Bach's "Jesu, Joy of Man's Desiring." Byron Yasui is a music theory and composition professor at the University of Hawaii. An award-winning serious composer, he also has serious ukulele chops that can be heard in his version of "Stars and Stripes Forever."

The New Generation

Since 1997, a whole new generation of ukulele artists has come into its own. Much of the finest work from this new generation joins the techniques of the prior generation with the songs and styles of current popular music.

Daniel Ho

The ukulele is just one of the many musical instruments that Daniel Ho plays extremely well. Growing up in Kaimuki, a small town on the island of Oahu, Ho studied many instruments including the ukulele. He began his professional career in 1990 as keyboard player, producer and composer for the contemporary jazz group Kilauea. Since then he has recorded many CDs as a solo artist. The 2002 release, *Pineapple*

Mango, features Ho's ukulele virtuoso side. He mixes smooth jazz originals with a Bach Invention and a brilliant arrangement of Dave Brubeck's "Blue Rondo a la Turk."

Herb Ohta, Jr.

The son of ukulele legend Herb Ohta (Ohta-San), Herb Ohta, Jr. has also become a highly respected ukulele artist. Born December 3, 1970, Ohta, Jr. grew up in Honolulu surrounded by the sound of his dad's ukulele. He also took formal lessons from his father until the age of twelve. In 1990, he was a guest artist on one of his dad's recordings and by 1995 he was showing up on compilation CDs like Paani Records *Ukulele Stylings #1*. In 1997, Ohta, Jr. released his first of

several solo CDs, *Ka Hanauna Hou*. He has been nominated for four Na Hoku Hanohano awards (the "Hokus" are the Hawaiian equivalent of the Grammy awards) and won twice. Ohta Jr. has also dedicated much of his time to teaching ukulele to others.

Jake Shimabukuro

To many observers of the current uke scene, Hawaiian Jake Shimabukuro is the one to watch. Still in his twenties, Shimabukuro has demonstrated an extraordinary mastery of the instrument, forging a style that has elements of classical music, flamenco, jazz, blues and rock. He first came to the atten-

Jake Shimabukuro

sunday morning

tion of the music world through his work in two Hawaiian pop groups, Pure Heart and Colon. On his 2002 solo CD *Sunday Morning*, he tackles the Paganini "Caprice No. 24," pop standards such as "Sleep Walk" and "Close To You," as well as his own smooth jazz and rock tunes. In the liner notes, Jake expresses a longing common to many of the greatest players, saying "I would like to represent the ukulele as best as possible and demonstrate how versatile the instrument can be."

THE U.S. MAINLAND

John King

With his 1998 CD of Bach compositions, John King makes a convincing case for the "classical ukulele." In 1960, while living in Hawaii, King began playing the ukulele after receiving his first instruction from his mother, an accomplished amateur. Following many

years of classical guitar study, he returned to the ukulele with a "new understanding and insight." King's CD is arranged for the unaccompanied ukulele and performed in the *campanella* style of the Baroque era, "a style noted for a bell-like quality of sound in which individual notes over-ring one another producing an effect very much like a harp. This is accomplished by playing each succeeding note in a melodic line on a different string." King teaches guitar at Eckerd College in St. Petersburg, Florida, and devotes time to his interest in the history of Hawaiian music and the ukulele. His book *The Hawaiian 'Ukulele and Guitar Makers: 1884-1930* (NALU Music, 2001) is a painstakingly researched look at the

Portuguese machête, the ancestor of the ukulele, and the early years following its introduction to Hawaii.

Janet Klein

As a young girl growing up in Southern California, Janet Klein loved to listen to old records of popular songs from the early twentieth century. It wasn't until she decided to learn to play the ukulele that she hit on a way to share the love of these songs with others. In 1998, she released her first CD, *Come Into My Parlor* and since then has released two more recordings. All of her CDs showcase her boundless enthusiasm for "obscure, naughty and lovely songs from the 1910s, '20s and '30s."

Examples include "Banana In Your Fruit Basket," "Nasty Man," and "Yiddish Hula Boy." Klein can often be found singing and strumming her Tony Graziano custom uke around California with her backup band, the Parlor Boys.

AUSTRALIA

Azo Bell

Based in Byron Bay, Australia, The Old Spice Boys feature one of the most unique uke players on any continent. After being a professional guitarist for many years, "Ukulelist" Azo Bell picked up the uke in 1992. With Billy Milroy on single-string or "tea-chest" bass and Tim Reeves on snare drum, the Old Spice Boys mix superb musicianship and a wacky sense of humor on jazz standards, vaudeville tunes and originals. Bell has a loose playing style that can sometimes disguise the fact that he is providing 80% of all the melody and harmony.

On their 2002 CD, *Alibi of Birdland*, The Old Spice Boys tackle "Maiden Voyage," "It's Only a Paper Moon" and "Take Five."

CANADA

Langley Ukulele Ensemble & James Hill

If you want to know what two dozen ukuleles picked and strummed together sound like, look no further than the Langley Ukulele Ensemble. Based in Langley, British Columbia, this group has taken their unique sound far beyond their home. The members of the group are all from the Langley school system, and despite their youth, are veterans of the road and recording studio. Under the leadership of energetic director Peter Luongo, the LUE has performed at Roy Sakuma's Ukulele Festival in Honolulu and toured Canada and the Mainland U.S. They've released sever-

The Langley Ukulele Ensemble

al CDs that feature a mix of Hawaiian, pop and jazz standards. While attending the University of British Columbia, Luongo discovered the teachings of Canadian ukulele educator J. Chalmers Doane and the LUE sound is influenced by the Doane-directed Halifax ensembles of the 'seventies and 'eighties. The Langley Ukulele Ensemble also continues the tradition of playing the triangular Doane ukuleles.

One of the stars of the Langley Ukulele Ensemble is James Hill. Hill joined the LUE in the fifth grade and continues to be the group's top ukulele virtuoso.

james hill playing it like it isn't...

In April 2002 Hill released his first solo CD, *Playing it like it isn't...*, which demonstrates his virtuosity on a wide range of material, including "The Flight of the Bumblebee," "Orange Blossom Special" and "Take the 'A' Train."

FRANCE

Ukulele Club de Paris

The seeds of the Ukulele Club de Paris began in the early 1980s. At the time, Cyril LeFebvre and Joseph Racaille had been raising eyebrows as a ukulele and steel guitar duo playing Schubert at events like the Zurich Jazz Festival. When they met Bradney Scott, an Englishman with a fondness for George Formby, the three decided to form a trio. The name they chose was inspired by the mandolin and accordion ensembles of Paris in the early twentieth century. In the early 1990s, after attracting several other Parisian strummers, the newly expanded group became regulars at art

gallery openings and fashion-industry events. In 2002, they released their first CD for Universal France, *Manuia*, which revealed a delightful mix of Hawaiian, French, English and American Mainland influences.

JAPAN

IWAO

Born in Yamagata, Japan in 1963, IWAO began his professional music career as a singer and guitarist at the age of 25. In 1991 he heard Herb Ohta peform in Honolulu and was inspired to take up the uke. Since then he has released many CDs that showcase his ukulele virtuosity, singing and songwriting talents. On his 2002 release *Postcard Summer* he mixes originals with pop standards like "Girl From Ipanema," "Around the World" and a

cool version of "So What" by Miles Davis. IWAO performs regularly throughout Japan with his group the Papaw Crew, and plays in Hawaii once or twice a year.

(CD COVERS COURTESY OF: NATIONAL ORGANIZATION FOR TRADITIONAL ARTISTS EXCHANGE, DANIEL HO CREATIONS, ROY SAKUMA PRODUCTIONS, SONY MUSIC JAPAN, NALU COMPACT DISCS, COEUR DE JEANETTE PRODUCTIONS, OLD SPICE BOYS, LANGLEY UKULELE ENSEMBLE, ukulelejames.com, UNIVERSAL FRANCE AND GEMMATIKA RECORDS.) OPPOSITE PAGE: BACKGROUND IMAGE: JANET KLEIN (COURTESY OF JANET KLEIN)

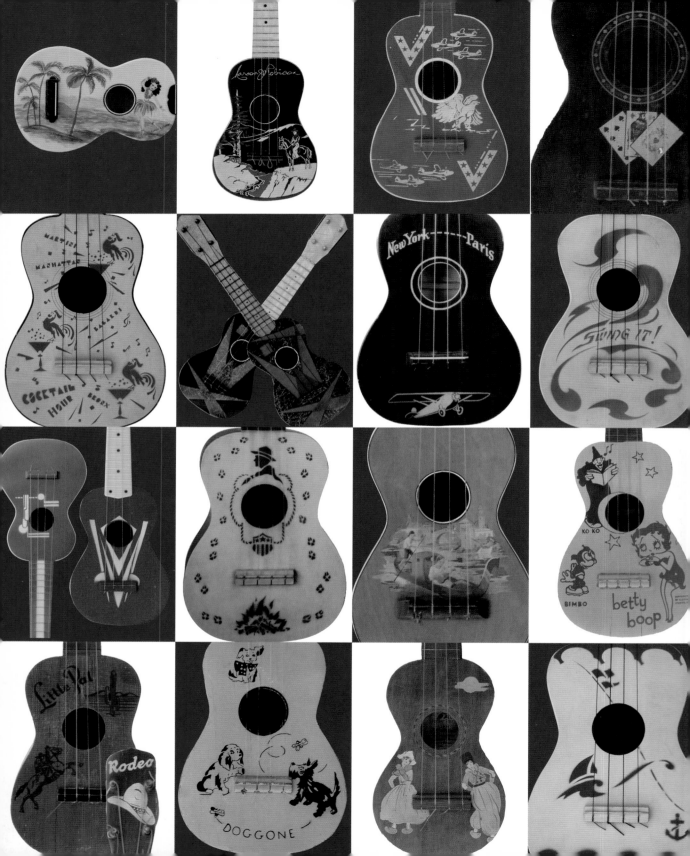

More Novelty Ukes

SINCE THE PUBLICATION OF THE FIRST EDITION OF THIS BOOK, VINTAGE UKULELES HAVE BECOME EVEN MORE SOUGHT AFTER. THIS IS TRUE FOR BOTH THE FINER HAWAIIAN-MADE AND MAINLAND INSTRUMENTS AS WELL AS THE NOVELTY UKES. PRODUCED PRIMARILY BY CHICAGO MANUFACTURERS HARMONY AND REGAL, THESE NOVELTY UKULELES FEATURED AMUSING DESIGN THEMES AND CARTOON CHARACTERS. PICTURED ON THE OPPOSITE PAGE ARE:

TOP ROW:

ISLANDER PLASTIC UKE HAND PAINTED ON FRONT BY CARRIE BREEN, SISTER OF MAY SINGHI BREEN

CARSON ROBISON SOLD BY MONTGOMERY WARD, CA. 1936-1940

REGAL VICTORY

FIRST HAWAIIAN CONSERVATORY OF MUSIC—PLAYING CARDS

SECOND ROW:

REGAL COCKTAIL HOUR

TWO ART MODERNE UKES

"LINDY" (COURTESY OF THE THE R.J. KLIMPERT COLLECTION)

REGAL "SWING IT"

THIRD ROW:

TWO ART DECO UKES

BOY SCOUT (COURTESY OF THE R.J. KLIMPERT COLLECTION)

LA VENECIA

BETTY BOOP

FOURTH ROW:

LITTLE PAL, CA. 1950

DOGGONE

"HAND PAINTED"

NAUTICAL

Today's Ukulele Makers

With the interest in ukuleles on the upswing once more, there has been a similar increase in the amount of ukulele makers.

CLOCKWISE FROM TOP: TODARO "SWEETHEART" (PHOTO BY SANDOR NAGYSZALANCZY)
NATIONAL UKULELE; A FLOCK OF FLUKE UKES; ANDY POWERS UKE
JAPANESE ALL PLASTIC "PINEAPPLE" UKE (COURTESY OF KAZUYUKI SEKIGUCHI).

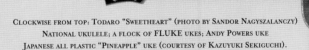

TONY GRAZIANO; AUGUSTINO LOPRINZI; JOEL ECKHAUS OF EARNEST INSTRUMENTS; DALE WEBB, DESIGNER OF THE FLUKE UKULELE.
(PHOTOS BY ELIZABETH MAIHOCK BELOFF)

TOP: "FRISCO UKE"

ABOVE: TENOR UKULELE DESIGNED
AND MADE BY DAVID HURD —
UKULELES BY KAWIKA, INC.

WHAT FOLLOWS ARE SOME OF THE MANY COMPANIES AND INDIVIDUAL LUTHIERS WHO ARE CURRENTLY BUILDING BETTER UKES.

Beltona
www.beltona.net
Specializes in resonator ukes

Black Bear Ukuleles
blackbear@nwinfo.net.
Fine conventional and unconventional ukuleles of all shapes and sizes

Earnest Instruments
www.earnestinstruments.com
Traditional, custom, and uncommon including cigar box, watermelon and rock 'n' roll ukes

H. F. Eibert Stringed Instruments
Hfe2@twcny.rr.com
Restoration and construction of stringed instruments

G–String Ukuleles
www.gstringukuleles.com
Top-quality ukuleles, all sizes, custom work

Gomes Guitars & Ukuleles
Kauila@kona.net
All size custom ukuleles using local Hawaiian woods

Tony Graziano Ukuleles
www.grazianoukuleles.com
Makes all sizes, specializing in tenor and baritone ukes

Hana Lima ʻIa
www.hanalima.com
Teaches ukulele making, custom-built ukuleles

Island Ukulele and Guitars of Kauai
www.koaukulele.com
All size custom-made koa ukuleles

KP Ukulele
www.kpukulele.com
All size custom-built ukuleles

Kamaka Hawaii, Inc.
www.kamakaukulele.com
Maker of fine Hawaiian koa ukuleles

Kanileʻa Ukulele
www.kanileaukulele.com
All size handcrafted professional and student-model ukuleles

KoAloha Ukulele
www.koalohaukulele.com
Specializing in koa concert and tenor ukes

Koʻolau Guitar & Ukulele Company
www.koolauukulele.com
Specializing in professional quality, custom ukuleles

Augustino LoPrinzi
www.augustinoloprinzi.com
All size mahogany, koa and custom ukes

The Magic Fluke Company
www.fleamarketmusic.com
Fluke and Flea ukuleles

The Martin Guitar Company
www.martinguitar.com
Backpacker and SO model ukulele

Mele Ukulele
www.meleukulele.com
Specializing in acoustic and electric 4-, 6- and 8-string koa ukuleles

National Reso-Phonic Guitars
www.nationalguitars.com
Original metal and wood-bodied resophonic ukes

North Pacific Productions
www.northpacificproductions.com
Rosewood tenor and baritone and koa soprano and concert ukes

O Kona Ukuleles & Guitars
www.ukulelesofkona.com
All size ukuleles using local Hawaiian woods

Pegasus Guitars & Ukuleles
www.pegasusguitars.com
Specializes in custom-made ukuleles

Po Mahina Ukuleles
www.pomahina.com
Island-style ukuleles

Andy Powers Musical Instrument Co.
Powersandrew@hotmail.com
Specializing in ukes of all shapes, sizes and tonewoods

RISA Musical Instruments GmbH
www.risa-music.de; www.ukulele.de
Specializing in electric ukuleles (the Uke Stick)

R.L. Saul Ukuleles
www.rlsaulukuleles.com
Quality concert ukuleles

Talina Banjo-ukes
www.ukuleleworld.com
Banjo ukes

David Talsma
ukefan@earthlink.net
Soprano/concert scale, especially pineapple-shaped ukes

3rd Wave Ukuleles
www.3rdwaveukuleles.com
Finely crafted ukuleles with laser-engraved art

Timberline Music Inc.
Timberline@webhart.net
Reproductions of the old Martin/Ditson models including style 5Ks

Todaro's Music
www.akulele.com
Akulele ukes carved from one piece of wood in the tradition of the Bolivian charango

Ukebrand Ukuleles
www.ukebrand.com
Soprano and concert instruments modeled on Kumalae and Martin ukes

Ukiyo Ukuleles
www.ukiyoukuleles.com
Specializing in all standard sizes plus reproduction Roy Smeck Vita ukes

Ukuleles By Kawika, Inc.
www.ukuleles.com
Specializing in concert, baritone and 4-, 6- and 8-string tenor ukes

Valley Made Ukuleles
www.valleymadeukuleles.com
All size traditional koa and custom ukes

Young Ukuleles
www.youngukuleles.com
Specializing in hand-crafted nylon and steel-string ukuleles

These manufacturers are testament to a healthy and growing contemporary uke market. While nowhere near as large as it was during the Hawaiian craze of the 'teens and twenties or the Godfrey years, today's market is filled with uke fans who are there for the long haul.

Any serious discussion of the ukulele naturally leads to a prediction of a "comeback." The problem with a "comeback" is that, like any fad, it can go away just as quickly. Perhaps the best one can hope for is a growing public recognition of the qualities that have made the ukulele popular since 1879: It is a small, portable instrument that is easy to learn, and yet allows for virtuosity. And, perhaps more than any other musical instrument, the ukulele can bring a smile to almost anyone.

THE PEGASUS 5-STRING TENOR,
AND HARRY EIBERT "HARP" UKE,
ARE JUST SOME OF THE UKULELES
BEING MADE TODAY.

Lee – thanks for everything. Lee Silva(L), Stan Williams(R), "The Wanderers," 1965.

Bibliography AND Resource Guide

HISTORY

Brooks, Tim; Marsh, Earle, *The Complete Directory To Prime Time Network And Cable TV Shows 1946—Present*. Sixth Edition, Ballantine Books, 1995. Information on Cliff Edwards and Arthur Godfrey television shows.
Brown, DeSoto, *Hawaii Recalls— Selling Romance To America*. Editions Limited, 1982.
Cabral, Elma T., "Grandpa Was A Troubadour." *Paradise Of The Pacific,* December 1946. Story of Augusto Dias, his voyage to Hawaii and his role in the invention of the ukulele.
Cabral, Elma T., "The Ukulele's Real Story." *Honolulu,* 1978.
Chee Tsutsumi, Cheryl, "Ukulele: The Strings That Bind." *Aloha,* March/April 1986.
Copland, Aaron; Perlis, Vivian, *Copland 1900 Through 1942*. St. Martins/Marek, 1984.
Elbert, Samuel H.; Knowlton, Edgar C., "Ukulele." *American Speech,* 1957.
Grove Dictionary Of Musical Instruments, The, Vol. 3, pp. 696-697, entry on ukulele.
Hawaii Book, The—Story Of Our Island Paradise (including selections from *Paradise Of The Pacific*). J.G. Ferguson Publishing Co., 1961.
Kanahele, George S., editor, *Hawaiian Music And Musicians—An Illustrated History*. The University Press Of Hawaii, 1979.
King, John, *The Hawaiian Ukulele & Guitar Makers* Nalu Music 2001
Nunes, Leslie; Felix, John Henry; Senecal, Peter F., "*The Ukulele—A Portuguese Gift To Hawaii.*" Offset House, Inc., 1980.
Phipp, Richard, "Is It Possible? A Serious History Of The Ukulele." *Guitar International,* November, 1990.
Reyes, Luis, I., *Made In Paradise— Hollywood's Films Of Hawaii And The South Seas*. Mutual Publishing, 1995.
Sackett, Susan, *Prime Time Hits— Television's Most Popular Network Programs— 1950 To The Present*. Billboard Books, 1993.
Spaeth, Sigmund, *A History Of Popular Music In America*. Random House, 1948.
Steele, H. Thomas, *The Hawaiian Shirt— Its Art and History*. Abbeville Press, 1984.
Tatar, Elizabeth, *Strains Of Change— The Impact Of Tourism On Hawaiian Music*. Bishop Museum Press, 1987.

PLAYERS

ASCAP Biographical Dictionary. Jaques Cattell Press; R.R. Bowker Co., 1980.
Crosby, John, "It's Arthur Godfrey Time." *Memories,* Feb./ March 1989.
Davies, Russell, "That Old Formby Magic." *Telegraph Magazine,* 4/20/91.
Guiness Encyclopedia Of Popular Music, The, Second Edition. Edited by Colin Larkin. Guiness, London, 1995.
Kiner, Larry F., *The Cliff Edwards Discography*. Greenwood Press, 1987.
King-Lenson, Margo, Editor-*Pacific Voices Talk Story, vol. #1*, 2001, Tui Communications. Chapter on Bill Tapia "Ukulele Jazz"
New Grove Dictionary Of Music And Musicians. Edited by Stanley Sadie, 1980.
O'Brian, Jack, *Godfrey The Great*. Cross Publications, Inc., 1951.
Pile, Stephen, "Ukulele Crazy." *Telegraph Magazine* , 12/23/95. Article on The Ukulele Orchestra Of Great Britain.
Randall, Alan; Seaton, Ray, *George Formby*. W. H. Allen, London, 1974.
Randall, Alan; Walley, John, *George Formby Complete*. Wise Publications, London, New York.
Sallis, James, *The Guitar Players— One Instrument And Its Masters In American Music*. William Morrow & Co., Inc., 1982. Chapter titled "The Wizard Of The Strings: Roy Smeck."
Stein, Harry, *Tiny Tim—An Unauthorized Biography*. Playboy Press Book, 1976.
Tiny Tim, The True Fantastic Story Of… Corncob Ltd, 1968. Fanzine.
Walsh, George, *Gentleman Jimmy Walker— Mayor Of The Jazz Age*. Praeger. Reference to Richard Konter.

MANUFACTURERS

Brozman, Bob, with Dopyera, Dr. John, Jr.; Smith, Richard R.; Atkinson, Gary, *The History And Artistry Of National Resonator Instruments*. Centerstream Publishing, 1993.
Brozman, Bob, "Martin Ukuleles And Taropatches."
Calabash, "The Return Of The Uke." *Honolulu.* September 1995.
Carter, Walter, *Gibson Guitars—100 Years Of An American Icon* . General Publishing Group, 1994.
Crescendo, The: A Monthly Publication Devoted To The Interests Of The Harp, Mandolin, Guitar And Banjo And Kindred Instruments. Column on "The Ukulele," by C. S. DeLano, 1917—1920.
Elder, Ben, "Born Again." *Acoustic Guitar,* January 1996. Article on Weissenborn instruments.
Evans, Steve; Middlebrook, Ron, *Cowboy Guitars*, Centerstream 2002
Glatzer, Hal, "The Ukulele." *Frets Magazine,* September 1980.
Gruhn George; Carter, Walter, *Acoustic Guitars And Other Fretted Instruments — A Photographic History*. Backbeat Books, 1993.
Horn, Yvonne Michie, "Jumping Fleas." *Islands,* July/August 1993.
Klimpert, R.J., "Ukuleles." *Vintage Guitar Classics,* Fall 1994.
Longworth, Mike, *Martin Guitars— A History*. Third Edition. Four Maples Press, Inc., 1988.
Sallis, James, "The Ukulele Instruments." *Pickin'.*
Simmons, Michael, "The Real Ukulele." *Acoustic Guitar,* November 1996.
Teagle, John, *Washburn—Over One Hundred Years Of Fine Stringed Instruments*. Music Sales Corp., 1996.
Wheeler, Tom, *American Guitars— An Illustrated History*. Revised and Updated Edition. Harper Perennial, 1992.
Witty, James, "Ukulele Craftsmen." *Pacific Connections.*
Wright, Michael, "The Guitars Of Mario Maccaferri— Part 2…Fantastic Plastics." *Vintage Guitar Magazine,* 1995.

JIM BELOFF

Jim Beloff is the author, compiler and publisher of over a dozen songbooks for the ukulele. He has also released CDs of original songs performed on the ukulele and made a how-to-play video entitled *The Joy of Uke*. In 1999, Jim and his family introduced a colorful and low-cost ukulele called the FLUKE that has won admirers all over the world. Jim and his wife Liz own Flea Market Music, Inc. a company dedicated to the ukulele. They believe very strongly that *"Uke Can Change The World."* You can reach Jim at www.fleamarketmusic.com.